The Welcomers
Stories of Reunions in Heaven

by
Maureen Morrell

Kingdom
Publishers

The Welcomers

Confronting and Comforting Your Losses Stories of Reunions in Heaven

Copyright© Maureen Morrell

All rights reserved. No part of this book may be reproduced in any form by photocopying or any electronic or mechanical means, including information storage or retrieval systems, without permission in writing from both the copyright owner and the publisher of the book. The right of Maureen Morrell to be identified as the author of this work has been asserted by her in accordance with the Copyright, Designs and Patents Act 1988 and any subsequent amendments thereto.

A catalogue record for this book is available from the British Library.

All Scripture Quotations have been taken from the New International Version and the King James Version of the Bible.

ISBN: 978-1-911697-04-6

1st Edition by Kingdom Publishers

Kingdom Publishers
London, UK.

You can purchase copies of this book from any leading bookstore or email
contact@kingdompublishers.co.uk

Dedication

I thank all the many people who I have been privileged to call friends over my 76 years.

Firstly, to my family for their love and support and to Sally for her bravery in the very early days.

To Tina, a steadfast friend, and latterly to Jane, who God brought into my life in the last few years to share some of the difficulties of living with Bi-polar and to give and receive encouragement to publish this book,

And last but not least, to Terry my husband for his support and practical help in collating this book.

I continue to pray for all who have suffered loss in any and all ways.

CONTENTS – INDEX TO STORIES

Foreword	9
Rachel's Story	11
Chapter 1	11
The Welcome – Rachel and Marcus	17
Chapter 2	17
Marian, Face to Face with God	22
Chapter 3	22
The Grandmother's Story	24
Chapter 1 – Serena	24
Chapter 2 – Simon's story	28
Chapter 3 – Serena Goes Home	30
Chapter 4 – Answers for Sandy	32
Katy's Story	34
Chapter 1 – Katy	34
Chapter 2 – Katy's New Body	41
Chapter 3 – Colin's Reunion	43
Donna	45
Chapter 1 – Donna's Story	45
Chapeter 2 – Donna's Haven	50
Chapter 3 – Donna's Mum talks to God	53
Lizzie's Story	55
Chapter 1 – Lizzie	55
Chapter 2 – Lizzie and God Talk	61

Chapter 3 – Lizzie dances with her Daughter.	63
The Twins	65
Chapter 1 - Twins	65
Chapter 2 – The Twins Meet Mum	69
Chapter 3 – Beth and God	72
Ginnys Story	73
Chapter 1 – Ginny	73
Chapter 2 – John's Life	79
Chapter 3 – Ginny and John	80
Chapter 4 – John, God and Mum	82
Irene	83
Chapter 1 -Irene's Baby	83
Chapter 2 – Tara's Story	88
Chapter 3 – An End to Anguish	90
Carol and Jim's Story	92
Chapter 1 - Carol and Jim	92
Chapter 2 – A Life in Four Acts	95
Chapter 3 – Not a Futile Life	98

Foreword

I have known Maureen over a number of years and always valued her input to the church.

I believe this book will bring some comfort and consolation to anyone who has suffered a loss.

Debby Wright
Pastor – Trent Vineyard, Nottingham

Rachel's Story

Chapter 1

"That's my mum" said Rachel "in the red coat – the one with the slightly greying hair".

"She looks tired" observed Kate.

Kate, her Guardian had been with Rachel from the beginning, all through the pain, she'd picked her up and together they had travelled to the place of safety where she now was, able to look at her mother with sadness and love

They quietly watched Marian as she sat on the bench at the cemetery. They saw her collect two containers which she filled with pink and apricot roses, silent tears fell onto the seat as she arranged them. She made no attempt to hide them despite the pitying glances of the other visitors to neighbouring graves. After a while she slowly rose and placed one container of pink roses at one side of a large Celtic cross, the case of apricot roses on the other side. The cross which stood at the intersection of two paths around the cemetery seemed a fitting place.

Rachel felt her heart hurting and reached out for Katie's hand – "They're for me, aren't they?" she said.

"Yes and for your brother – it's taken so long but I'm glad she's been able to do that at last.

"Lay me to rest you mean", Rachel suddenly felt lighter as if a huge weight had been taken off her shoulders – "it's been so long" she sighed "twenty eight years".

"She asked for your forgiveness before she placed the flowers at the cross. Are you able to do that?". Kate knew this was the hardest question she'd ever asked Rachel – but knew how much rested on Rachel's answer. Even in Heaven where there was no sin, the words of forgiveness still needed to be said when there had been no chance on earth.

"I know I ought to but not sure if I can right now – seeing her has brought so many memories back to me. Can you leave me alone for a time Kate?"

Kate had things to see to which would occupy her for most of the day, Although she'd been with Rachel from the beginning and would be her friend for eternity, she knew that Rachel needed time. She had seen great progress through the years, but this was a strategic breakthrough for both Rachel and for her mother. As she went on to her next task she prayed for the eventual reconciliation of mum and daughter in Heaven whenever that time might be.

Rachel walked round for a while enjoying the sound of the river as it trickled over a waterfall. It was quite narrow here before it met with other streams heading to the main river. She found a clearing on the banks where she could see both ways up and down the stream and somehow Rachel knew that to begin to look back she needed to know she could also look forward from there.

She still remembered it all so clearly, every tiny thought and feeling etched into her memory bank. She recalled the moment that her mother found out she was pregnant and that anguished cry and stomach lurching fear which the knowledge produced in both mother and in herself. The fear which grew and grew from the discovery of the pregnancy and on through her mother's desperate telephone conversation with her father and the fateful words – "I don't want another child – you can have an abortion". Rachel didn't know what that meant only that it struck fear into her mother and herself.

Rachel's breathing increased and her heart started thumping, pumping blood around her ears blotting out the sound of the stream.

She was back there in that confined space hearing and feeling again the panic and anxiety of her mother which communicated itself at first as a bitter rejection of her by her mum and then increasingly as terror at the full horror of what was intended.

"Why don't you want me mummy? I'll be no trouble".

Rachel who had no voice sobbed in anguish at what was being contemplated about her fate. But Rachel knew that her mother couldn't hear her above the clamour of her own fears. Perhaps if she lay there quietly her mother would know she would be a good baby and change her mind. Fear mounted in Rachel as she was aware of plans being made for something called a 'termination and though she didn't exactly know what this was, she knew it concerned her and was causing her mother to be filled with anxiety.

Rachel didn't think her father had been around much – she hadn't heard him in the house, only her mum speaking on the phone to him occasionally, talking about money to pay for this 'termination'.

She'd been with her mum for 14 weeks when one morning they left the house with a suitcase and caught a train to Manchester. Rachel knew mum was crying all the way there and people kept asking if she was alright.

Immediately they entered the 'Clinic' Rachel heard the sounds. She recognised voices crying for help, and knew they were babies like her and soon her voice would be heard along with theirs. Rachel had no fists yet to pound her mother with, but she screamed as loud as she could – maybe her mum would hear, maybe she would change her mind.

As she strained at the traumatic memories being unleashed Rachel felt the warm sun on her face and reached down to the velvety grass on which she sat. It brought her a little more courage to continue and to finished reliving the events as she remembered she was now safe, loved and wanted here in Heaven.

She suddenly doubled up in agony and looked around to see who had come up behind her and kicked her in the back. Then she remembered the pain of being evicted from the warm security of the womb before she was ready, before was grown, before she was...

RACHEL, RACHEL, the voice called from somewhere nearby. She felt herself drifting somewhere soft, which after such pain was wonderful. Where was that voice – she looked around her – the mist cleared – she was in a park.

"Hello" the voice that had called her name from out of the mist spoke "I'm Kathryn (Kate for short), I've chosen to look after you for ever here in Heaven and I've been waiting for you to arrive. Come on I'll show you around.

Rachel began to take in her surroundings, the park had several dedicated areas, one was a playground – another for children to play with animals which she noticed were there and yet another complete with comfortable seating where there were around a hundred or so children with their heavenly carers taking lunch or having a hug.

Overwhelmed by the feeling of love and safety here in the park, Rachel put her hand in Katy's as they watched. "You'll get to know some of the others soon I'm sure, they have all come here through the same route was yourself, but each of you has been specially chosen by a guardian and will be in their care for ever.

Rachel was confused – it had all happened so quickly – suddenly she was in a different place. Kate said "I'm taking you to meet the only one who can make sense of things for you. He's in charge of everything".

The room where they were to meet someone called 'Father' was so beautiful, but the 'being' who emerged at the entrance to the room was beyond description, a radiance that gave off every good thing, love, purity, compassion, righteousness, justice and peace. Rachel knew that this was GOD. And God was speaking to her.

"Rachel, come here".

As her eyes adjusted to the brightness surrounding God, she slowly went towards Him. As she approached, she saw a few other children playing around His knees. "Come" He said again and lifted her onto His knee. "I want to tell you how special you are to me and how much I care that you've been hurt".

Rachel then experienced her first ever hug and as she looked, she saw Katy smiling at her – her friend and guardian here in Heaven.

Rachel felt the dampness through her fingers of the grass beneath her. She was suddenly aware that it was raining gently – just like her mother's tears. She knew she was in the best place ever and was sad to know that her mum was still going through hurt and pain. Rachel knew that she wanted to see her mum eventually when she arrived in Heaven, she wanted to hug her, to tell her she forgave her and to ease her pain, but that would have to wait.

Kate always knew the right time to turn up – here she was strolling along the riverbank. Rachel told her straight away of her journey into the past and she was ready to throw her stone. Kate had taught Rachel well over the years and whenever they needed to talk, they'd sit and throw stones into the stream. As they talked Rachel threw her stone and said "I forgive you mum and I can't wait to see your face, I'll be waiting for you".

She looked up to see a wonderful smile on Kate's face. "Our Heavenly Father will be so thrilled. Now I've something to tell you which has had to wait for this day – because this is a special task which you can now undertake. You know you have a brother here, called Marcus, who arrived under the same circumstances as you, we would like you to help him prepare to meet your mum when she arrives".

"I wonder if Marcus ever sees mum" Rachel wondered aloud, "I'd like him to make peace with her before we both meet her".

As Kate filed her report that evening, she did so with mixed emotions, as she knew she would now be given another 'major' assignment and that Rachel who had grown up into a beautiful woman was now ready for her own 'assignments'.

She took one last look at Rachel's mother – who had walked away from the cemetery and stopped by the river in the town. Here she bent down and picked up 2 stones and as she threw them into the water she said "This is for you Rachel and Marcus" and as she watched the ripples spread out she knew she had been completely forgiven and that she would see them both again.

The Welcome – Rachel and Marcus

Chapter 2

Marcus looked intently at Rachel. She knew something, he was sure of it. Her face glowed and her eyes flashed with excitement. He couldn't ask her anything as just at that moment they involved in the Welcoming Ceremony of a newcomer, but as soon as they were on their own he would question her. He wondered what it could be. Rachel sometimes helped prepare the lists of those who were expected to arrive shortly – it could be that she had seen a name she knew. The ceremony was coming to an end, it was always a glorious time for everyone to be part of. To see Father embrace the newest arrivals and no one would ever tire of feeling once again the love of that first meeting.

People began to wander away afterwards, although a few stayed sitting on the grass and talking with their friends. Marcus and Rachel had many friends here, but since they had met in heaven and realised, they were brother and sister they had asked to work together. They had been assigned to 'signwriting' as they were both very artistic and had such enjoyment creating wonderful posters, signs and programmes for the many events which took place every day around Heaven.

"Rach" Marcus hesitated. He didn't want to question her unnecessarily or put her on the spot but "Is there anything you want to tell me"? Rachel smiled "I wondered when you'd notice, it didn't take you long, but I just can't keep the good news to myself any longer. I know we're not supposed to divulge the names of people who are imminently expected, but guess who's coming fairly soon"?

Rachel continued to babble "Of course you don't have to even guess, there's only one person who we even knew on earth and that's our mother".

Rachel suddenly stopped, remembering how she had needed to come to terms with her feelings towards her mother. Marcus had lost the smile and was looking into the distance towards the golden pathways and further into the golden city. She put her hand on his arm "Marcus, I'm sorry, I should have realised it would be a bit of a shock to you".

"It's OK Rachel, it's a surprise that's all. I have known it would come and have been trying to prepare myself. My guardian, Sebastian has been slowly guiding me to think about this for some time, but I suppose I hadn't realised how I'd feel when it became a reality".

"How do you feel, Marcus?" Rachel asked. "Could you greet her in forgiveness or do you need time? It would be lovely if we could both welcome her, but I totally understand if you aren't ready for that". Marcus agreed "I think I do need to get things straighter. I'll find you later today and let you know. How soon will she arrive, do you know"?

"I think we're talking days rather than weeks, she's been very ill and she's tired. I'll meet you later".

Rachel walked towards Kate's house. Kate was a good friend, always there, although very busy in her guardian duties with the many babies who continued to arrive.

"Kate", she sighed "My big day is nearly here".

Kate knew immediately what Rachel was referring to, she had seen her through all her growing years in Heaven and into the maturity she had now achieved and knew this next act of acceptance was crucial for her. Kate also knew that she was almost ready for promotion to Guardian her own new babies.

Marcus wandered towards the golden paths he loved, the Highway to the City, it was this very vista that he had first glimpsed when he entered Heaven. The only comparison he had to the golden light was the light which had violated his being when he was expelled from his mother. Although, he thought, that was the shock of hurt and pain and this, this glorious light had immediately brought warmth and healing, love and such joy and peace to his soul the moment he encountered it.

Sebi found Marcus sitting on the little hill overlooking the City and quietly sat down beside him. "I knew Marcus, I've just seen the list. Your mother is due tomorrow afternoon, will you be able to welcome her do you think?

Marcus took time to phrase the words which were forming in his heart and mind. "Somehow I know that as I hug her then I shall know that I've forgiven her, and she will know she is forgiven too. I've been thinking – who knows what I would have been and done on earth. I might have been really terrible, hurting people, you know all of the diabolical things we hear in our news from earth. How dreadful that would have been to live with so, yes Sebi I'm ready to welcome her, I can't wait in fact".

Sebastian, like Kate when Rachel had made great strides in her growth, now glowed with pleasure.

Rachel and Marcus were both kept very busy the next morning, although their rota had been changed to allow for the afternoon's momentous events, and in fact the next few weeks had been designated as holiday time so that mother and children could spend time together.

Lunch was a picnic taken very near to the Admin Office so that they could go straight in and watch events as they unfolded on the screen in the office.

At 2pm they knocked on the door, Peter, who never seemed to sleep was there as usual. "Come in" he growled; his voice still had the deep tones of the fisherman about it. He directed them to the viewing gallery where anyone who wanted could see their friends and families enter into Heaven.

Marcus and Rachel adjusted their eyes to the viewing screen and found themselves looking into a small but comfortable room with a bed and some homely books and ornaments around. Rachel noticed some lovely pictures on the wall and pointed out to Marcus some of the colours and it struck her that both she and her brother had inherited their mother's artistic genes.

The woman in the bed was smiling as she talked with another lady at the side of the bed who was holding her hand. It occurred to Rachel and Marcus simultaneously that they did not yet know their mum's name.

"Her name is Marian" said Peter.

"Who is the lady at her side?" asked Rachel

"That's your sister, Sarah" answered Peter – another surprise for Marcus and Rachel.

"She looks very sad" Rachel observed. "She's having to say goodbye too, we know what that's like don't we Marcus". Marcus' eyes filled with tears.

Heaven only saw welcomes, never goodbyes so tears and hurts were not felt here, but they both recognised the feelings in Sarah's heart and they asked Father to ease the pain for her. Marian touched Sarah's head and told her she loved her and thanked her for all she'd been as a daughter and that they'd would meet up in Heaven. Rachel and Marcus were both moved by this. Then she appeared to doze off for a few minutes.

Marian's lips began moving slowly and gently and it was obvious that no-one in the room could hear her, but Marcus and Rachel could hear the words she was saying. She was praying to Father that she might see Him soon.

Peter began to move some dials and keys on the computer. "Is she coming now?" Rachel asked. He moved to another screen with the well known and loved gates which were slowly opening. Rachel and Marcus moved their seats so that they were now concentrating on this screen. "When can we see her?" Marcus asked "As soon as she comes through the gates?"

Peter said that he mostly welcomed people on his own but that sometimes children needed to be reunited with Mums and Dads quickly and it saved a lot of admin.

As they watched, they saw a figure walking up to the gates, she strode slowly but with confidence and as she caught sight of Peter waiting, she began to run until she was almost in his arms. Peter laughed and hugged her.

Marcus and Rachel couldn't hear what was said but Peter beckoned them to come forward. Marian didn't need to be told who they were, Marcus and Rachel looked into Marian's eyes and together said "We love you mum". They hugged and smiled and hugged again so much that Peter had to ask them to move out of the gateway!

Kate and Sebastian came to take them to the mansion where they were to meet and celebrate with many friends this wonderful reunion. The whole place was decorated with vines and flowers and tables at the side for the subsequent banquet were overflowing. The music was unlike anything Marian had ever heard.

Then the singing increased and the dancing began – Marian, Rachel and Marcus began the dancing, and then went to sit by Jesus' feet where they held hands and began their new lives in Heaven.

Marian, Face to Face with God

Chapter 3

"How are you settling into your new home, Marian?" Marian could hardly speak for the knowledge that his was God who addressed her. She was still marvelling at the fact that she had two audiences with God one on her arrival and this one.

"It's more beautiful that I ever imagined" she answered. "I know You told us Heaven would be wonderful, but we never knew what perfection was on earth".

God spoke– "When people first arrive it is all so new and overwhelming and when we met on your arrival, I embraced you so that felt forgiven and accepted. Today I want to let you know how much I loved you and was shaping events in your life when you got things wrong"

Marian nodded – she was still amazed at the fact that there were no more tears to be shed and that even now when Heavenly Father was going through her life there would be no sorrow or grief, just a deeper understanding of the mind of Father and His love.

"Do you remember looking out of the train window travelling back from the first abortion. You were tracing the path of the raindrop as it slid down the window, pushed along out of control events and I saw your heart, heavy and tear sodden both then and through many years as you remembered the pain. I longed to tell you then that it would be alright one day".

"Yes I do remember, how could I forget? My heart was as heavy as lead".

"It was then I planted the seed of compassion in your heart that would grow through the years identifying with the shame, hurts and sorrows of others. Even though I knew you may make the same choice again the following year. Jesus my Son was praying that you might not, but I couldn't take that freedom away from you even though it caused my Son and I such sadness to watch you".

Marian had known that not every person shared quite the same depth of compassion for hurting people that she did and often wondered if it was because she had been into the deep herself. She looked up at Father and He touched her face.

"I always saw your potential, and even through your struggles with all your weaknesses, I and many others whose lives you touched knew you to be a channel of My love and care".

Marian's heart was bursting with love and joy with all that Father was saying. She saw a smile spread across His face.

"I've a surprise for you" now he laughed out loud, "I do love this part" he chuckled.

"Another party is about to start where you will be my guest, my Son and I call this celebration the Reunion of Friends. All the people whose lives you've touched with My love are waiting for you now. Can you hear the music is beginning. Come".

Through the door was an exquisite Banqueting Hall filled with faces all turned towards them and all applauding the entry of God. God turned towards Marian. "I'll leave you now, this is your celebration, enjoy and accept the joy of those you showed My love to".

He bent down to embrace Marian and the applause swelled through the hall again.

Marian turned to the room, faces half-forgotten beamed at her. She'd remember their names when they talked together. This was going to be some party!

The Grandmother's Story

Chapter 1 – Serena

It was a Friday again, a reprieve for Serena – 2 days away from the grind of the treadmill of the office. How she loved 4pm on a Friday and how somehow on Sunday it landed on her almost like a tangible weight on her shoulders as she contemplated Monday again. She then made a mental effort to push the weight aside for a few more hours and concentrate on the good things in her life. Her daughter Sandy was one such good thing and the joy of her living within a 10-minute journey instead of 3 hours before her move, was enough to lift her spirits.

'Grandmother' she rolled it round her head – then said it out loud and laughed at the picture that conjured up. 'Zimmer frame – shawl – knitting – cats'. No, not Grandmother, grandma or Granny, I think – if Sandy prefers of course.

"I really don't know where the time has gone" Serena had been telling her colleague over lunch the previous day. "I certainly don't feel old enough to be a gran, but I know I'll enjoy it. I'm so looking forward to bouncing babies and spoiling them, then handing them back when they need changing.

Serena spent the evening pottering around the house and letting her mind wander over the new course her daughter's life would take, and her own too. It would give her a new lease of life, she knew – it could sometimes be lonely without a husband.

Monday was quite bright once the mist had lifted, and as usual Serena was breakfasting 'on the hoof' a slice of toast in one hand and lipstick in the other. It never ceased to amaze her how some women could make up on the bus, train or coach – she had a difficult enough time getting a straight line on her lips, only manageable with her specs on.

The phone trilled, Serena bristled, "Who on earth is phoning at 8.15, don't they know I have to be out of the house in 59 seconds? If it's double glazing, they'll certainly start their day with an ear full!"

"Hello" barked Serena into the offending instrument. "Mum" Serena's stomach fluttered, the voice was wrong – Sandy was always bright and full of the joys of spring or any season. She always cheered Serena when she was down. "I'm losing the baby". The stomach ceased fluttering and turned over, she felt sick, but somehow said the right thing. "Yes I'm on my way – have you called the doctor? Have you phoned Simon?" Too many questions – just go Serena.

'Oh' ....thought Serena, the office, I'll have to call in, that'll take a few more precious minutes'. They were pretty understanding, although behind the immediate sympathy ran the unspoken words, the hidden agenda – 'Don't be off too long, we'll have to get a temp in, you already had a day off sick 3 weeks ago and you've a week's holiday soon'. 'Stuff them!' thought Serena as she put the phone back and grabbed her coat.

The journey to Sandy's although usually short, proved a hasstle with rush hour traffic, really heavy, Serena put a tape on of soothing music, it did nothing to calm her or concentrate her mind on what the next few hours would bring. Her mind was foggy, confused, blanked, already feeling the pain of loss, remembering again the losses in her own life. Tears flooded Serena's eyes and she slowed the car to wipe her eyes and nose.

Then she was there, and her mood changed, it had to, this was her daughter who needed her to be strong. And she was strong, she took complete charge, calmly arranging with the doctor for Sandy's admission to hospital, although it seemed to have been a very quick miscarriage – she would still require some medical attention and checks. Simon, who was serving in Northern Ireland was devastated when she spoke to him. Serena had to wait while the Sergeant located him as he was not on duty. He'd ask for compassionate leave to come home and be with Sandy for a few days but was not sure if he could swing it. Serena heard the tremble in his voice and wished she could put an arm around him, he was more like her own son than son-in-law.

Sandy's doctor said she'd be OK to go in the car to hospital, so Serena drove the four miles into the county Maternity Unit with a knot of iron in her stomach. Now that they were alone Serena was at a total loss – what did she say – there was nothing at all except "I'm sorry love". Sandy said, "I know mum". Serena had never heard her voice so flat and lifeless.

She saw Sandy into her room, thankfully a private one, and there she was swallowed up in procedures, nurses, blood tests and pressure, machines for this and that.

She went to the cafeteria; the nurse had told her to come back in the afternoon to visit or to take her home. Serena actually wandered round town for several hours, she couldn't remember where, but ended up looking in the window of a baby shop and filling up with tears. She arrived back to find Simon had come straight from his plane in a taxi and was sitting with Sandy and kissing her hand. He said, "Doctor says she can go home in a couple of hours".

Serena said how sorry she was again to Simon and mumbled something about hoping and praying for the next time. She stumbled out of the ward in tears and tried to find her way to the exit. The sign ahead was blurred, it wasn't the exit, what was it -Oh the Chapel. Serena hoped no-one was in there, she just needed to cry and cry out to God. It was quiet despite the noises of the surrounding corridors, she collapsed in one of the front chairs and sobbed her heart out. Then suddenly she felt very angry with God.

"That's my baby in that ward who is hurting that she lost her own baby, my grandchild, You've taken my grandchild away". Serena poured out all her grief of the day's events and the other losses of babies in the family which still hurt.

When she began to calm down, she noticed it had begun to rain and grow dark outside, so she switched on the lights and blinked, blinded by the sudden dazzle. She noticed the room for the first time, the altar had a gentle light cast upon the cross and a simple bunch of just opening daffodils. 'New life' she thought, 'not for Sandy's baby though, but perhaps new hope. Can I dare to hope God'? This was directed at the ceiling. Serena walked up to the altar where a Bible was open, she hadn't much time for church now, but she did believe (when she needed to, like now), but had a lot of respect for those like Sandy and Simon who had a solid faith and secretly wished she too could believe in something or someone firm and solid who wouldn't let her down.

The Bible was open at Jeremiah 29 v 11 and highlighted were the words in chapter 29 verse 29 – "I know the plans I have for you, plans to give you a hope and a future".

It seemed like a light had gone on in Serena's heart just like the cliches she'd laughed at in the past, but so true. She had to sit down. Someone had answered her, was it God? – It had to be. Logic told her that many would read the same words coming into the Chapel but today Serena knew these words had got further than just her mind, they had gone deep into her soul to lift her. She felt quite different going out of the hospital. Almost happy, but no that wouldn't be right – joyful perhaps and certainly more hopeful for her own future and for Sandy when she came home and recovered.

Serena opened her front door and walked down the hall. She threw her coat onto the chair knocking something onto the floor. It was her breakfast toast. Tears threatened again and she started to fight them, but realised she must let them out, there would be a time to laugh again, God had shown her that in the Chapel.

Chapter 2 – Simon's story

Simon stood at the back of the church. A confusion of feelings raced through his system. Embarrassment, anger, a hard knot in his heart refused to shift. People were drifting by and glancing at him, someone laid a hand on his arm which he shook off by taking a step backwards.

Sandy didn't need him there as she was at the front of the church on her knees, crying and praying with her friends around her. It slightly embarrassed him that she should draw attention to herself and their situation in that way. He hated too much attention, he didn't know what to do when people offered sympathy and love except shrug it off. He was very angry with God for allowing his child to die, it was a simple as that and he couldn't move the feeling and then, he had to praise God and worship Him. Somehow, he was still able to do that at one level while deep down there was a seething mass of hurt. He'd kept it together for Sandy he'd been strong and when she'd asked if he'd cried or grieved at all he'd given her a vague answer.

Simon felt a hand on his arm again and tried to take another step back and away. It was Joe, an older man who Simon hadn't spoken to very often. It was generally thought that he had quite a few problems of his own. He often went forward for prayer at the end of the service.

'What can he have to say to me, that will have any relevance to our situation?' thought Simon 'he's a single man who has no idea what it's like to lose a baby, how on earth am I to respond to his offer of prayer?'

Simon stiffened and became even more aware of people coming and going around him and he was about to be prayed for in the middle of an exit! Joe didn't say a word, just stood with his hand on Simon's shoulder quietly praying. Simon couldn't hear the words, but he began to get warmer and closed his eyes. 'Maybe I'll feel less inhibited if I can't see people?' He felt a warmth spreading through his body, he'd never experienced this before, although he'd prayed for people where this had occurred. This was something else though, his whole body was glowing, and he could hardly stand, it felt as if a weight was pressing him to the floor but the warmth he felt was melting his heart and he let it take him. He knew he'd fallen onto the floor and he heard a soft crying sound which grew in intensity until he realised it was his own cries. He let it happen until his deep moans and cries turned to gulped sobs. As the tears dried he began to hear words, some he knew were from Joe, but others were directly into his mind.

"You're a whole man"

"You are a good husband"

"I love you just as you are, not as you believe you should be, or for what you can achieve".

Simon stood up and lifted his hands to receive all the good stuff, words and love which poured over him from God.

After a while he opened his eyes and smiled around him. Two of his friends had quietly joined the pair and stood nearby. He knew that God had been healing some deep wounds and as he looked over to Sandy he saw that she had been watching and their smiles said they'd now be able to talk of their loss and also to look ahead at what the future would hold and to laugh again.

Chapter 3 – Serena Goes Home

The time had arrived, Serena knew – she was so tired and ready to go.

It had not been a long illness, but her body had been slowly malfunctioning, as her grandson had put it and although she was grateful and blessed by her family and friends who visited and prayed with her over the weeks, she knew she would not recover in this world.

Each morning brought a deep sigh from her, as she realised the heaviness of another day trying to be brave when she so wanted to be with Jesus, to have complete rest for her soul and body.

Today though, was it, she knew when she woke. The pain was not so severe, and there was an easing of the leaden effect of her body. She drifted off to sleep and was dimly aware during her doze of voices in the room but sounding very far away. She inched her eyes open and saw Sandy very close to and lifting her hand.

"Is this it then?" she whispered as Sandy bent to hear her.

"I think so mum". Sandy lifted Serena's hand to her lips. "I love you mum you've been so good to us all".

Serena's limited vision took in Simon standing behind Sandy and the two grandchildren, Caitlan and Seamus. Serena was so pleased Sandy had continued the Irish heritage of her family by the naming of her children. So here they were gathered at his side, she felt happy, how strange. She managed a smile. "I'll see you all soon – you know that".

Sandy laughed gently, "Well not too soon mum, I hope".

"Take care of my precious grandchildren". Serena beckoned them over and they bent to kiss her.

"Bye gran". Seamus said with brimming eyes.

"See you in Heaven gran" Caitlan squeezed Serena's hand. Caitlan had been a lovely visitor for her while she'd been ill – coming and reading the Bible and praying for her or just relating events of her social life and allowing Serena to reminisce about her own.

Serena closed her eyes, she could let go now, all was well.

Even before she opened her eyes, she knew she was somewhere different. Her body was light, no pain, no headache from all the drugs and a floating sensation. Her eyes opened and she realised she was moving, being led along a very bright passage. She could see the door ahead and someone opening it for her and going ahead.

Once through, Serena took a huge breath of clean, clear, pure air and blinked in a sunlight she'd never experienced before.

The person who opened the door now approached. She thought she knew him but couldn't quite think who it was.

"I've come to take you through the gates and into Heaven and to show you your new home there. Do you know who I am?"

Serena examined his face, it had the eyes of Caitlan and the broad forehead of Simon. "Oh" breathed Serena "you are the grandson I never saw", she cried in joy. "I never even knew what sex you were, what's your name?"

"I'm Kieran. At the naming ceremony Father said he knew my mother would have chosen an Irish name for me".

Serena knew the best was still to come, meeting Father and Jesus but her cup of joy was almost flowing over now.

She stepped lightly at the side of Kieran, each step getting more like the step of a young spring lamb as she neared the throne of God.

Chapter 4 – Answers for Sandy

Through Sandy's mind passed all the questions she had wanted to ask God when she arrived in Heaven. She needed to ask them before she was reunited with her mum and her baby.

"Why, why and why – what had I done wrong – what had my baby done wrong – what about all those who chose to kill their babies by abortion of abuse?

The years between the loss and her mother's passing had been good years, sharing the joys that God had promised the family in the hospital that day, and the life she and Simon had together after the children had left home had been wonderful.

Now the time had come to meet with Father, the steam that stoked the engine of unfairness had run out, and since she'd arrived, she'd met with so many whose stories were horrific which simply put hers into proportion.

She walked into the Presence Chamber and gasped as she experienced for the second time the mystery that is God.

Father patted the chair placed at His feet and Sandy sat down.

She had so much to say but didn't know where to begin.

"I know how hard you found living without an answer to your questions and still having faith to believe that I was a good God. I want you to know how much I loved you for that and for bringing up your family to love and serve Me. They bring me such joy".

Sandy's heart swelled with pride with joy and love that Father was proud of her.

"But I will tell you about your son Kieran – I know you've met him. Although the medical staff would not have found anything wrong with him, it wasn't possible for him to be born. There was a defect that they wouldn't have known about. How would you respond now though if I said I wanted to take him home for your sake and his. That I knew you'd grow close to me through the trauma?"

God looked intently at Sandy and she softly responded.

"I've always known you are a God of love in my head and although it would have taken some time I think I would eventually been able to say like Mary – "May it be unto me according to Your will".

God smiled at Sandy.

"You have been a good and faithful servant to Me and to your family and friends. Well done!"

Katy's Story

Chapter 1 – Katy

Katy slithered down the slide, her dress around her armpits, shrieking with laughter. Landing at the bottom she hobbled round to the steps again, most of her friends overtaking her as she was having difficulty propelling her body as fast as she wanted to.

Jenny, Katy's mother wiped away a tear which refused to be blinked away as she watched her beautiful, sweet natured child enjoying a few moments of normality playing with other children. She'd had to carry her from the car to the park, but Katy had been determined to enjoy this morning's sunshine playing with her friends before she went back into hospital.

Even here the questions came 'Why, why, why my child, why not that little boy who's bullying and punching his sister – why my Katy?'

"Jarvis" yelled the boy's mother sitting next to Jenny, "Gerrof yer sister".

Another tear came and a snuffle.

"Hayfever?" asked Jarvis' mum "My sister Rene suffers wiv it sumfing awful".

"No" lied Jenny "Just a summer cold". She stood up and called "Come on Katy love, we'd better get back".

"Mummy, do I have to go back to hospital tomorrow, can't I go when daddy gets back?" Katy looked hopefully up at her mum as they drove home hoping for a reprieve. She'd knew there was none really, she'd been in and out of St Matthews Childrens' Hospital so often, but this time she wanted to prolong her stay at home.

Jenny knew that this time it was more serious, the last scan had shown that the bone cancer had spread from her legs into her spine and the pain and immobility were getting worse each day. The doctors had told Jenny only last week that there was nothing more that could be done for Katy, as she had received the maximum treatment possible. Pain relief was now the priority and Katy needed something much stronger than the painkilling medication Jenny administered at home.

Katy, at five years of age was a remarkable child, having been diagnosed with the disease at the age of three and spent at least half of each subsequent year in hospital, charming all the staff with her infectious laugh and mischievous sense of fun. She got that from her dad of course. Jenny stifled the sigh that often accompanied her thoughts about Col.

She and Colin had married within six months of their first meeting and Jenny's family questioned her hasty decision. Colin was a quiet man and Jenny loved that in him, sensitive and gentle, everything that her previous boyfriends were not. It was when he was working away two years ago that she noticed a change in him. Not that he had become less kind and loving, but he became 'religious'. Jenny blamed it on his sister and brother-in-law who he visited at weekends when he was away. He didn't say much at first, but she noticed that he would go into the bedroom on his own about half-an-hour before they usually went to bed and she discovered him reading his Bible. Another time she'd found him on his knees in the living room when she needed a drink in the middle of the night.

They had always talked about Katy's illness together, discussing the prognosis and what it would mean to them if she died, but this last year had been difficult, even hateful because she felt Colin had gone away from her, had somehow deserted her. Oh, he talked about God and Jesus and what they meant to him, but somehow that seemed to make it all the worse. He loved them more than her obviously! He tried to tell her that she too could have this peace, but while Katy was so ill there was no peace for Jenny. She might believe if there was but otherwise, no, it wasn't for her, all that having to be good – and anyway how could God love the world and still allow the pain that Katy and so many others suffered. No, Col was not the Col she had married.

Colin sighed as he walked out of the church with his sister, Sue and her husband. Why couldn't Jenny see that accepting God into her life would make facing Katy's illness and whatever the future would bring so much easier with the knowledge that there was hope at the end of this life for all of them. The atmosphere at home was getting worse, even though he was praying more for Jenny and especially Katy.

He rang home as soon as he reached his hotel room. Jenny answered straight away as Katy often slept very lightly and the phone often work her.

"Hi Jen", "how's Katy?"

Oh, Col she's managed a trip to the park today, but that's done her completely, she flaked out when we arrived home.

"I'm so sorry, I can't be with you tomorrow when she goes into hospital, I'm not able to get away before Wednesday afternoon, so I'll be home in the evening." The pause at the end of the phone told Colin that Jenny was very upset.

Jenny didn't really want to talk about how she felt, or how she thought Katy felt, it was all too much. She'd just go from day to day without too much thought, because then she wouldn't actually feel!

He told her about his sister and her family activities to lighten things and Jenny responded in the same vein by telling him about her parent's holiday plans. The conversation seemed to come to a full stop with so much unsaid and so much tension in the air and Colin finished as always with "God bless" before putting the phone down.

As Jenny wakened Katy next morning, she could see how ill she'd become. Her colour was like putty, and it took every ounce of her energy to get out of bed and allow Jenny to dress her. The pain was immense causing her to cry out as Jenny put her socks and shoes on.

Katy hated actually going into the hospital doors but as soon as she arrived on the ward, she was fine, quickly re-establishing friendships with the staff and finding out who was on the ward, who was new and who an old hand like herself. Her favourite sister was on duty – Julie, so she was very pleased. All the children were allowed to call staff by their first names and Sister Julie greeted Katy in her usual loving manner.

She hugged her gently and told her she'd got a smudge on her nose and to wash it off!

Katy laughed and pulled Jenny's hand dragging her towards Sister Julie – "I haven't got a smudge on my nose have I mummy? Julie says I have". Jenny laughed with Julie "No, I just think you need a tissue to wipe your nose".

"Ugh" Katy pulled a face "Have I got a snotty nose then?"

They were still giggling together as Julie showed Katy into the side room assigned to Katy for her stay. They all thought in terms of this stay, even though at the very backs of all their minds was the thought that this might be her last. Jenny always stayed most nights in the same room as Katy, but that evening she couldn't sleep and spent nearly two hours tossing and turning that she knew would eventually wake Katy, so she made her way to the parent's room and slept there.

Mr Stevens, Katy's consultant met with Jenny at 10am next day. The timing worked well for the children because they could watch childrens' tv or a video. The moment she walked into Mr Stevens office she knew it was very serious news. Sister Julie and another woman who was introduced as Ann Brown, a paediatric counsellor all stood up as she the room. Mr Stevens indicated for all to sit. Jenny's legs began to shake as she lowered herself on to the chair.

He began as Jenny knew he would, with the words "I'm so sorry Mrs French". The next words seemed to fade away and Ann thingummy said gently, "We'll explain when you're ready Jenny".

It appeared that Katy was entering the last stage of her illness for which there was now no cure and that her vital organs could fail at any time. Mr Stevens and the staff were extremely kind and gentle in all they said but somehow even though Jenny had been expecting this some time, she was not prepared for this loss of feelings. She thought she would cry out, yelling as they did on tv dramas. "Oh no, not my child" or similar words, but this cold, cold clamp round her heart was worse. How could she face Katy, how would she react to her child who was going to die so soon?

"Hi mummy" Katy's eyes stayed on the tv – it was her favourite programme, always making her laugh. Jenny sat down and watched with Katy, eyes glazed as the characters on the screen acted away oblivious to the fact the her daughter was dying. How dare people laugh, she looked around at another set of parents who were enjoying the show with their young son. He looked healthy, thought Jenny, he'll be home with them soon. She watched Katy laughing, then pain suddenly gripped her, and she called out.

Julie administered the necessary pain relief and Jenny lifted her back into bed. "Mummy" murmured Katy as she drifted off to sleep, Jenny's stomach churned, she's going to ask me how she really is. "Am I going to die soon?"

Jenny couldn't face it, not just now. "Sshh, go to sleep now, darling, then the pain will go away". Katy drifted off and Jenny went over to the window. She stood for over an hour looking out of the window, watching life pass by, cars full of people, children, girls just like her Katy, all full of life.

Around 5.30pm Katy stirred just as Jenny had brought her cup of tea and a sandwich from the café. "Mummy". Katy's speech was slurred "I've asked Jesus to bring daddy here so I can say goodbye". Jenny wanted desperately to tell her not to be so silly, that she wasn't going to die and anyway prayer didn't work.

"Yes dear, go back to sleep now". Jenny almost choked on the words. Her daughter knew and accepted what Jenny was not able to face up to.

Jenny woke with a start and felt damp spreading around her knees. She'd nodded off her half-drunk cup of tea over her legs. "Damn, damn, damn". She mouthed the words and the tears started silently to ooze out of her eyes and trickle down her face. The door opened and Colin took in the whole scene, Katy asleep, and Jenny's tears. He took her in his arms and held her, rocking her back and forth like he did with Katy when she was upset. Slowly the tears subsided, and she let her head rest on Colin's shoulder. There was simply no fight left in her.

An hour later Katy woke, and it was immediately obvious that although she was thrilled to see her dad and mum there, she was in excruciating pain. Jenny rang the bell for Julie as Katy managed to say to her dad. "I asked Jesus to bring you here".

"And He did, shall we ask Him to be with you now?" Colin was aware of Jenny standing behind him but knew this was what Katy wanted.

"Yes, please daddy". Colin prayed that Jesus would take away her pain and that she could be with Him and free from pain.

Julie explained that Katy now needed the strongest painkiller to ease her through, and that she probably wouldn't be very coherent from now on. Colin took Jenny's hand as Julie administered the medication. It worked immediately and Katy's face lost that strained look.

Colin and Jenny took turns to sleep, and it was about 4.30am when Katy stirred and looked up at the ceiling, then at Colin and Jenny.

"Can you see the stars, have they taken the roof off the room. I can see the stars in the sky and a man dressed in white is giving me His hand – shall I take it daddy? Is it Jesus?"

"Yes Katy". Colin took her hand and Jenny her other- "Mummy and I and holding your hands here in this bedroom but Jesus will take your hand and lead you up to the stars".

Katy died peacefully at 4.40am on Monday 18th June, it said so on the Death Certificate that Jenny now held in her hand. It had been so sudden at the end, she hadn't been prepared for the swiftness of it and now she and Colin had to go and bury their darling daughter.

Colin had spent time with her being kind, gentle and loving, but somehow it didn't get through the coldness, and he needed some comfort too. He was glad that Katy hadn't asked Colin if she'd see both of them in Heaven. Colin knew that only time would tell on that one, but he could look forward to that day as he stood in the gentle summer rain, as their daughter was lowered into her earthly resting place with the eternal words of the Committal:-

Death is swallowed up in victory

And he could fancy he saw her little mischievous smile as she darted among the stars, playing hide and seek with Jesus.

Chapter 2 – Katy's New Body

Colin was totally right about Katy's new life. Her favourite game was hide and seek and she loved to dart in and out of the trees lining many of the streets in the City.

They had trunks that shone, and she loved to see the branches reflected in the pavements below. Sometimes she would play the game with her guardian, Leah, but often with anyone she could find who was passing by, but mostly she loved to stand and gaze at the brilliance of the whole scene.

When she'd arrived, she could not believe the lack of pain and the fact she could run and jump freely. She spent a lot of time talking with Leah about her mum and dad and of her life of hospitals and pain and that she was looking forward to seeing her mummy and daddy together again one day. Leah listening to Katy's bubbling chatter knew how important it was for her to do this before she met Father God.

Today was her day for meeting Father but Leah couldn't find her anywhere. She'd looked in all the usual places, the golden road into the City, around her favourite tree hiding places. 'Where could she be?' thought Leah. She heard the waterfall and made her way there through the lovely overhanging willow trees so beautiful with the glorious heavenly light making the branches shine like Christmas illuminations. Leah smiled at the thought, it was Katy herself, who had said that the shining brightness in the City was just like Christmas every day. Father would love to hear that.

As she approached the waterfall she walked more slowly, the sight always took her breath away. If the trees and the streets and buildings shone, then the water as it cascaded down and splashed into the large deep pool was beyond a description of brilliance. It was dazzling yet didn't hurt her eyes. The sound of water as it threw itself over the edge thundered but was not an assault on the ears and the feel of the water on the skin was such of a silken quality that it felt like soothing oil.

Leah quietly approached Katy as she didn't want to spoil that enjoyment.

"Hello Leah" Katy splashed some water Leah's way and laughed.

"It's your time to meet with Father God Katy, it's a good job I brought a change of clothes for you". Leah chuckled "Somehow I thought you'd be somewhere getting nice and messy!"

Katy asked many questions on their way to the Receiving Room "Would it just be God"? Where would Jesus be? What would the room be like? What did He look like?"

"Katy, stop, stop, stop, here we are, you'll know very soon. Each person's time with Father is individual and special and you can tell me all about it.

Leah spoke with Sarah who was the doorkeeper of the Receiving Room for that day. "Hi Katy, shall we go in?" Katy's heart began to beat faster, this was so exciting and a bit frightening. God sounded so much bigger than Jesus and she stepped tentatively into the Room.

Chapter 3 – Colin's Reunion

It was hard for Colin to say goodbye. For so many, many years he'd prayed that Jenny would become a Christian, that they would eventually have a life which could be shared on the spiritual level as well as the physical. His Christian family and friends were always such a support to him, especially after they'd lost Katy, but with the subsequent births of Christopher and Ben, Colin knew how hard it was for Jenny with that support, having to battle along with the fact that although they now had two lovely sons, there was no daughter to enjoy and share 'girly' things with.

She'd sometimes get out the photo albums and look over the early photos of Katy, but even that hurt because the comparisons between albums of the boys on holidays, playing on the sand and as a family group, made the individual photos of Katy either on her own of with Jenny, look sad and lonely.

They had both thought that their marriage would end with Katy's death, because of unspoken guilt and resentment and pure grief, and for a time Colin had stayed away more weekends than necessary picking up what support and comfort he could from the local church. But before long he became aware that God was asking him if he was willing to be in for the long haul with Jenny, whether she became a Christian or not, reminding him of his marriage vows and gently encouraging him to begin really working at loving her as she was.

It had it not been easy all of the time, but somehow, they had made a reasonably good family life, Colin knew this.

Now Colin knew that his own illness was going to take him home. The very thought of Heaven, being with God and seeing Katy always lifted the pain and guilt he felt when he knew he had cancer too. The guilt, because it was probably this cancer gene which he'd passed onto Katy, and he worried for the boys.

Jenny held his hand and stroked the side of his face gently, even his facial muscles now ached now at the slightest touch. It was agony to be washed and have his needs attended to and the morphine which he needed was taking away all of his mental functions. He only recognised Jenny and the boys. Others visited, his Pastor and other church friends, but he didn't know them anymore.

It was around 12.00pm that he left the bed he was lying on, he actually felt himself being lifted out and walking away, and he was so ready to go, he knew that even Jenny would not want to keep him here in this pain. As he walked from his life to the next, he asked God to look after Jenny and the boys, and that He would continue to love them and draw them to Him.

So, it was at 12.05pm that he walked up that same Golden Street which his daughter had so enjoyed playing on. There was a young woman walking up the road towards him, he could see her shimmering reflection in the gold pavement and as she approached his heart gave a lurch. Could it be?

"Daddy" Katy was about 20 yards away when she called out to him, she couldn't wait for him to come any closer, she had to run to him. The gap closed as Colin gathered momentum and suddenly realised that he could run and was forever free from pain and disability. The moment of meeting was more full of joy than they could ever have imagined and Katy led him to one of her favourite places so they could sit and talk.

They both spoke about her mum and Katy said she'd ask for a special Angel to visit with Jenny and let her know they were both happy here. They both hoped that someday she would join them, but for the moment it was sufficient that they had found each other and would enjoy all Heaven's delights.

Donna

Chapter 1 – Donna's Story

Donna lay very still in her cot. She'd woken up like most nights to hear the back door flung open and her father lurch through. She could feel herself tighten into a ball and put her fists up to her ears. This gave her the feeling that she mightn't hear whatever went on downstairs and that she could sleep through the night. She sucked her thumb and began to hum a little nursery rhyme her mum had sung as she put her to bed – "Humpty Dumpty sat on a wall – Humpty Dumpty had a great fall – Oh no not that one – Incy Wincy spider – that's better.

"Are you in bed you lazy slut? – get back down here and make my ..... supper". Sharon, Donna's mum was recovering from a particularly bad attack of 'flu' and several bruises to her head and neck which were taking longer to heal now her resistance was low. At least she had been able to spend some of the day in bed recovering because her neighbour had called and offered to take Donna out to the shops and park.

She had looked hard at Sharon as she stood in the doorway. "He'll do for you one of these days lovey, he wants locking up, he does! I nearly called the police". Mrs Jenkins patted Sharon's arm. "Oh no, we were just having a bit of a row" Sharon laughed weakly. "Steve was just a bit cross because I hadn't been able to wash his favourite T-shirt, and then I fell down the stairs". "Oh yes". Mrs Jenkins had heard this familiar story before and know there was no point in continuing the charade. She popped Donna into her pushchair, deciding to feed and change her in her own home and Sharon was thankful of the time to sleep away the reality of her life for a couple of hours.

Mrs Jenkins brought Donna back late afternoon and put her to bed for a rest as Sharon was obviously sleeping.

But reality soon returned for Sharon. Her stomach lurched; the familiar nauseous fear gripped her innards. She hadn't heard the front gate, or the door. 'Oh God'! She attempted to jump out of bed to get downstairs and give Steve his dinner but fell back onto the bed, her head spinning. 'If he comes up the stairs to find me it'll be worse than ever'.

From the next room Donna heard the sharp intake of breath and the low groan as her mother slowly raised herself from the bed and towards the door. As she passed Donna's door, she shut it tight whispering "Go to sleep sweetheart – it'll be alright".

Sharon had reached the top of the stairs and was starting down slowly holding onto the rail, she felt so giddy and ill, grasping the banister rail to stop herself from falling she sank down onto the top step. Everything seemed to be coming from a long way off, even the sound of Steve's cursing and then heavy footfalls along the hallway and up towards her on the stairs, each step causing her stomach to flip and her already trembling legs to feel like jelly. She wanted to pass out and away from it, but she knew she wouldn't be able to.

Donna had a tummy ache and her nappy needed changing. Today had been nice, although mummy wasn't there, she was in bed 'poorly' again. Mrs Jenkins from next door had taken her to the shops and the park, where she could sit in her pushchair and watch the leaves blowing and hear the birds in the treetops. Mrs Jenkins had talked to her all the time. Mummy didn't do that very often. Mrs Jenkins pointed to different things on their walk and explained what they were – "Look Donna, a puppy is chasing a ball, just look at him run straight past it – silly mutt!". She laughed and Donna's face broke into smiles even though she didn't really understand all that Mrs Jenkins said.

When they got back to Mrs Jenkins house, Donna had her lunch and her nappy changed. This was lovely, because mummy sometimes forgot when Donna was hungry, and especially if she wasn't well forgot her nappy too. Donna very often had to cry and cry before her mum noticed.

Donna, back in her cot, rocked and hummed but through the wall the familiar rising sounds cut through her song and as always it made her tummy feel bad and her head fuzzy. She knew the sequence that events would take, and her body tensed, and she started to whimper.

It suddenly went very quiet downstairs. – 'Good daddy's having his dinner' she thought 'he'll be happier now'. But then she heard the footsteps coming up the stairs – they were not her mother's, each step was heavy, accompanied by wheezy breathing and swearing (her mother called it 'cussing'). Donna didn't understand the words, but they sounded horrid, like the witches in her Fairy Story book. Then her door was flung open. "I bet you've had your meals today – so what are you whinging for". Donna's tummy hurt her more and she started crying louder. She didn't understand why daddy didn't like her or mummy and why they had to be hurt.

But daddy did like her, didn't he? Donna remembered the day mummy had said daddy loved her. Daddy was on holiday for a week from work and mummy said we could go to the seaside in the morning.

But daddy wouldn't get out of bed the next day and mummy had to wake him. Donna could hear her quietly asking him to wake up because it was late.

Daddy didn't like that and there was a lot of noise, shouting and thumping from their bedroom. Mummy was crying and then Donna started crying because mummy crying was bad! Daddy crashed into Donna's bedroom and broke her mobile of teddies and he stamped on them.

He shouted in Donna's ear, "It's your fault that she wants to go to the seaside", and his hand smacked her across the mouth. It hurt and she screamed which made him hit out again. Then Donna stopped and sucked her fingers.

Mummy came in later and got Donna up, washed her and told her that daddy loved her really.

That night was worse. When he got in from the 'pub' whatever that was, he hit the light switch in Donna's room with such force that he crushed his hand on the wall and swore violently kicking the door. The light hurt Donna's eyes – she'd never seen daddy this cross before. "Shut it will you? – I can't stand the noise – it's doing my head in. I'll ..... well shake you if you don't shut up". Donna closed her eyes tight as her father's face loomed above the cot, then she was being yanked out by her arms. She heard her mother coming slowly up the stairs begging "Leave her alone, she's only a tiny little thing, please don't hurt her".

"I'll teach her to keep me awake at nights with her crying – I'll show her who's boss in this house". Donna thought she would break in half from the shaking back and forth and then when she thought it had finished her father banged her head on the side of the cot. "That should show her". He snarled as he fumbled from Donna's room and into his bedroom, the need to collapse on the bed overcoming at last the desire for violence.

Donna's mother crept into her room and scooped her up. "Oh, my poot baby", she quietly crooned as her tears fell onto Donna's limp little body. "Please be alright – please be OK – he didn't mean to really hurt you. Just get some sleep and tomorrow will be better, you'll see".

Sharon wished she could stay with Donna and love her better, but experience had taught her that if Steve didn't get what he wanted before he fell asleep, she would get even more pain, so she eased her aching body into the bed, hoping against hope that Steve would be asleep before he realised she was beside him. But it was a forlorn hope!

Donna remembered feeling the pain stop. It was like the lightbulb that had been swinging crazily backwards and forwards inside her head for all of her eighteen months, had suddenly been switched off. For a moment it was quite dark and she was a little frightened, but then instead of that lightbulb there was a gentle glow which at first looked like a candle glow or like the night-light mummy had once put beside her bed until daddy swiped it away and told her not to be so stupid as to be afraid of the dark. The light gave her a very safe feeling.

Chapter 2 – Donna's Haven

There had been asked so many questions Donna has asked of her guardian after she had arrived in Heaven. She thought she would weary her, but Amy was always ready to listen and patient even when she couldn't answer the question. She had asked Heavenly father at their first meeting her most burning question "Why did daddy hurt mummy and me, why did he shake me so I died?"

Father had lifted her onto his knee and stroked her hair and shoulders and answered softly:

"Donna, your daddy didn't hurt you because he hated you, he really hated himself for being so horrible and because he couldn't hurt himself, he turned to the ones closest to him, that was you and your mummy. I know you also want to ask me why I couldn't stop him doing that and it is difficult to explain in a way that you will understand. But people on earth have to make the choice between being good and bad and your daddy chose being bad. It is only in Heaven that everything is good, and you can now enjoy all that."

Father knew that Donna needed to understand about her short life, so He told her how much He loved her and had longed to hug her, to tell her how much He had wanted to wipe her tears away. Donna snuggled close into Father's lap and fell asleep with a smile on her face.

Since then, Donna had grown with the help of Amy and for many years had been helping her to talk to other babies and children who had been hurt and killed by people on earth. She met many, who like her could not begin to understand why anyone could hurt them because they were so little and helpless and especially those who had been abused by family members, and she spent many hours just listening to their stories and helping them to understand by explaining what Father had told her when she arrived.

The latest baby to arrive, Fiona, needed quite a lot of time. Donna spent many hours sitting with her on Her knee and gently stroking her. Fiona knew that she was now safe, she'd met Father and felt happier than she'd even been but still needed to talk about her mummy who had hurt her and why her daddy had left home, so Donna and Amy between them were caring for her while she settled down in her new haven.

As Donna was walking with Fiona in the meadows and picking flowers, she saw Amy approaching – "Hi Amy, look at these lovely flowers Fiona has gathered." said Donna.

"They are beautiful Fiona" said Amy, "would you like to pick a bunch for me?"

Fiona happily applied herself to the task, kneeling among the wonderful meadow flowers and burying her nose in them to smell the fragrance.

Amy put her hand under Donna's elbow and guided her to a shady spot under a tree where they sat down. "What is it"?

Donna enquired – "Is there someone else you want me to help"?.

Amy paused before giving Donna the news.

"Your mum is coming to join us soon. I'm afraid your dad has beaten her, and she is badly hurt – she will probably be with us in a few days. I know you've spoken to lots of others who've been hurt, but how do you feel now about meeting your mum?"

Donna was honest. "At first, I couldn't understand how she could let this happen to me and although Father had explained about daddy, it took quite a long time before I could forgive my mum for letting it happen, but now I know I have done and after talking with many others, this has helped me understand that people are often not strong enough to stop the abuse because they are so afraid themselves. So, yes, I am ready to meet her and want to tell her it's alright and that I love her and want to see her as happy here as I am".

Amy was thrilled to hear Donna voice her feelings, she knew Donna had helped so many others like herself but did not know how she might react to meeting her mother. Amy explained to Donna the events of welcome which she remembered from her own arrival and excitedly they began to talk about the coming party.

When Donna arrived at the Palace of Celebrations, she saw that gathered all around the doorway were the babies and children she had helped over the years, they were looking at her, all smiles, because she was going to be the first one to meet her mum and they all wanted to share her happiness.

At first, she couldn't see her mum as there so many Angels, guardians and singers surrounding Father and Jesus on their thrones, then a pathway cleared and she could see her mother kneeling at the feet of Jesus. God reached down and took her hand, gently turning her around to see Donna at the doorway.

Donna walked towards her, noticing as she went the smooth, unblemished skin, the wide clear eyes, no longer blackened by bruising and fatigue and the shining blonde hair which she had never seen on her mum. She was beautiful. They met and as Donna reached out to touch her mother's hair, her mum too ran her hands through Donna's golden locks. For a while they didn't say anything, just looked at each other and smiled.

Then the celebration began, and they danced and danced together under the smiling gaze of all of Heaven.

Donna beckoned to all her friends in the doorway to come a join them, each one lifted their arms to Donna's mum for a hug, they were having a taste of their own coming reunions and Donna stood and smiled, then their smiles turned into a wonderful cascade of laughter and the joy of Heaven came upon them all.

.

Chapter 3 – Donna's Mum talks to God

She was still adjusting to having a name – Sharon. For so long on earth she'd just been 'Steve's missis' then of course 'Donna's mum' with the nudge of the elbow and the knowing look that followed that remark and the whispers – "You know the one who let her child die!"

Sharon's reunion with Donna had been tender – she'd never known before – the lightness of touch, the gentle smile, the kind words she'd heard since she had arrived were so foreign to all she'd known on earth.

When she'd first met God all she had wanted to do was gaze at Him, so totally tongue-tied that she was so pleased there was to be a second meeting, where she'd me able to tell Him how much she loved Him and simply being here.

And suddenly, here He was – touching her hand.

"I know you have so much you want to say to Me". God smiled down as Sharon sat at His feet. "So go ahead".

"I've never been so happy, I didn't know what it was" – it bubbled out of her, simply fizzed out "It's like the very best kids' outing possible with candyfloss and rides, only better".

"That's a lovely way to describe our life here, it is like the very best children's party. I planned that atmosphere to be here for you Sharon because I knew you'd never had a real childhood yourself. There were no parties for Gladys' kids were there?"

"No" Sharon thought about her childhood, the deprivation not only material, but emotional and spiritual, no-one told her about God, and Jesus was a swear word at her school.

God put his hand over Sharon's hand.

"Steve never knew what a good wife you could have been – despite your own upbringing, your heart is gentle and kind, there was a great capacity to bring that kindness to children. I knew that fear drove you to keep silent when you felt Donna was in trouble that night and how you suffered after her death.

I have a special task for you in Heaven – how would you like to organise all the children's parties in Heaven? I need a new co-ordinator, someone who will have wonderful ideas to bless the little ones. I'm sure we can make candyfloss in Heaven" He smiled. "it might be more like manna – but you are the very person we have been waiting for".

Sharon felt her cup was overflowing, her mind already buzzing with ideas. She reached out and hugged her Heavenly Father around the knees with both arms. He laughed again, that mixture of a chuckle and a rumble and placed His hands on her head.

"I'm so glad you are here". He said.

Lizzie's Story

Chapter 1 – Lizzie

Lizzie tried to raise an eyebrow – she tried this every day, along with trying to blink her eye to communicate that she did understand everything going on around her, every conversation, every look passed between the doctor to nurse, daughter to son-in-law.

"Why?" she screamed silently, "why am I still not able to control my body after all this time, three months since the stroke, so humiliating, frustrating and so damned unfair".

The medical staff had stopped trying to measure any sort of progress and she was simply now only having her bodily needs attended to, most of the nursing staff had stopped talking to her as if there was nobody at home!

Tuesday were Lizzie's best days, Molly was her nurse for that day, and she treated her with dignity and talked to her constantly, often about her own family, little bits of chit-chat, sometimes about the weather but most especially Lizzie enjoyed the little bits of Nursing Home gossip that Molly told her. She'd told Lizzie about Spike last week, being sacked after being found asleep in different places around the home, once in the linen store, once in the basement, where he'd been sent to investigate rodent activity and best of all in Matron's office during a night shift!

Lizzie appreciated Molly much more than her family, for hard as they tried, after five minutes telling her the latest family news, they'd fetch a magazine, or worse still when her grandchildren visited, they'd talk about their love lives as if she wasn't there. She suffered many emotions at these times, first anger at her family for being so unfeeling, then frustration that neither she nor the medical staff could make them see that she could hear and understand, then finally despair and the silent unshed tears which washed through her soul.

Occasionally Molly told her about her weekends which were always pretty chaotic, with her four children, but which nearly always revolved around some church activity on the Sunday. Lizzie loved to hear Molly's stories about the Sunday School Molly helped with, and the antics of the children.

Sometimes some of the things Molly told her touched her deeply, like the time she talked about a friend of hers who had lost a daughter to cancer. She spoke about the funeral service at her church and how her friend and family had been so brave, that they knew their daughter was now in Heaven and they wanted to rejoice that she was now out of pain. Lizzie could identify with this, she so wanted to be out of the pain of her semi-existence.

The Wednesday after Molly had told Lizzie this story, she woke with a strange fuzziness around her mind. She couldn't quite remember where she was or what she was doing there. Her bed was angled so that Lizzie could see out of the window, and she could see that it was very early and still dark.

She drifted off again, she was never sure if she closed her eyes when she went to sleep, but the next moment she was wide awake and 19 again standing looking out of the window of her Aunt Sarah's house in Yorkshire at the mist as it rose from the garden. Her Aunt would be waiting with the cab to take her into the Nursing Home run by the Nuns for the sole purpose of parting mothers from their newly born infants with the minimum of fuss and the swift dispatch of the mothers back to the bosom of their families with the stern warning, to never stray from the straight and narrow again!

Aunt Sarah didn't say much in the cab, even though Lizzie's labour pains were now coming strong and very painful, but she daren't make too much fuss because Aunt Sarah would utter her standard reply,

"Well young lady, you've got yourself into this mess, you'll just have to go through it".

The Nuns ushered Aunt Sarah into a waiting room, a cheerless room which matched Aunt Sarah utterly. Lizzie was swiftly marched along to a room to await her delivery. The niceties of a welcome or some sympathy for her pain were denied to anyone who found themselves in such a degrading position.

She gave birth at 9.24pm – the day had stretched into infinity, and at times the pain had caused her to pass out – she wished she could stay there out of the pain but always the voice of the Nun called Sister Mary would rouse her and bring her back to face the interminable pain. She heard the cry of the child and then passed out.

When she woke, she found herself in a different part of the Nursing Home in a room with other girls.

She called to the Sister "Where's my baby – what sex is it, can I see it?" The girl next to her turned her back on her as the Sister came up to the bed.

"It was a girl, and she's been taken straight to the adoption ward, you won't be able to see her, it's for the best".

Lizzie heard the girl in the next bed sobbing quietly and understood the heavy quietness of this ward – each girl carrying the weight of her grief and misery and knowing that under the same roof lay the babies they would never see.

Lizzie was pushed out within a few days of the delivery, once she had been declared fit – she didn't go back to Aunt Sarah's, she couldn't face the sour looks anymore and simply wanted to put as much distance between herself and the memories of Aunt Sarah's town as possible.

When Lizzie awoke, she felt a heaviness, and at first wondered if she was beginning to feel again. As she became more awake, she realised that she felt constricted around her heart, as thought she was going to have another attack, maybe this time it would take her, she hoped so. Her heart ached and she remembered the dream, the memories that had come flooding back, so vivid, she had almost been there.

"Oh, where did my baby go, is she still alive, has she had a good life, what is her name, Ooh God".

Lizzie heard the door opening and in walked Molly.

"But this is Wednesday, what are you doing here"? Lizzie silently questioned Molly.

"Hi Lizzie" said Molly, "I've changed my next week shift to today as we are going on holiday on Saturday, so you've got me two days running, sorry". Lizzie was not sorry, she was so pleased to see a friendly face on a day when she had reached back into the hurtful past.

Molly buzzed around getting Lizzie changed and washed, performing the menial tasks with care and loving attention and chatting as usual about her family.

"I visited with that friend last night, you know the one I was talking about to you yesterday, Lizzie, who's just lost her daughter. Well, she is amazing, she was telling me that she knew her daughter was in Heaven, and she would see her there one day because she believed that God would reunite all those who knew Him here on earth.

Molly suddenly stopped chatting and looked at Lizzie, "Lizzie, it's just occurred to me that you may not know that God loves you so much and wants to live in your heart. I don't know if you are a Christian or believe in God, but He loves you, just as you are and wants you to be with Him in Heaven. You know there is another life after this, and if we know and believe that Jesus is the Son of God, ask Him into our lives then when we leave this life, we'll enter into Heaven, and I believe we will meet all those we love and who love God. I would love to meet you there, free of this body of yours that you can't control. I would like to see you dancing and skipping for joy".

Molly was holding Lizzie's hand, "Please ask Him into your heart Lizzie and tell Him you're sorry for not coming to Him sooner and ask Him to make you new inside".

The door opened a notch.

"Molly, sorry to trouble you but we need you on Ward 3 right now, there's a bit of a crisis", one of the carers pushed her head round the door and then scurried away.

"I'll come and get you up as soon as I've finished there, Lizzie love. God Bless".

Lizzie looked up at the familiar crack in the ceiling which ran from the centre pendant light along to the pelmet at the right of the window, that was about the limit of her vision when she was on her bed. Well, she'd say the words to God and just see. Here goes.

Lizzie felt warmer suddenly, she wondered if the heating had been turned up, maybe there was a frost today, but she sort of glowed. She became aware of the colours of the wallpaper on the opposite wall, she hadn't noticed before that the pink was quite so vibrant, not garish, but rose coloured and that the ivy had different coloured veins on the leaves. Her eyes tried to stretch towards the door, because she was sure she had felt someone come into the room, but no-one spoke.

However, the feeling that someone else was with her in the room grew steadily along with the dawning knowledge in her heart that this was Jesus – God – in the room with her. Could she talk to Him? Was it allowed? Well, she would anyway.

Lizzie began to tell the presence in her room all her sorrows, hurts and especially about the baby she had to give up.

"I know You know all about her, and You must know where she is, so all I can do is ask You to make her a Christian so that I can meet her again in Heaven, please God. I know I've left it a bit late to ask, but

Molly always quoted the Bible where You said, 'Ask and you shall receive', so could I see her in Heaven with You?

Molly pushed open the door of Lizzie's room about an hour later.

"Here I am again, so sorry you've had to wait so ...." Molly looked down at the bed, Lizzie's eyes were closed – they never usually closed and the look on her face, well Molly just knew – the look was beautiful, so peaceful and full of joy. Her mouth had actually turned up in a smile, the face which for the last three months had not been able to move a muscle. Molly took Lizzie's hand in hers and took a few minutes before calling Matron just to thank God for Lizzie and to think of her meeting with her Father and walking towards Him her arms outstretched. She knew nothing of the request Lizzie had made or indeed about her daughter, but she knew that a crossing over had been made that day.

Chapter 2 – Lizzie and God Talk

"Why are some people so hard and unfeeling, Lord"? Lizzie launched straight in with her questions. "I've never been able to understand how they can be so cruel".

God looked down at Lizzie.

"It breaks My heart to see My world in such torment. And I would so love to stop it all this minute and change hearts forever, but how can I Lizzie, that would take away every bit of freewill, and how would I know people really wanted to love Me if I made them. With freewill comes the possibility of choosing evil and some make that decision early. I know that you're thinking of your Aunt Sarah who was so insensitive to you. But you know she was acting out of fear of what people would say and think of your family, if they knew you were pregnant without a husband. And fear motivates much of the evil, fear of losing face, fear of losing money or possessions. I do know you've forgiven her and although she didn't make it to Heaven, she always felt bad about her treatment of you."

Lizzie hesitated – she was asking Father so many questions, it seemed impertinent.

"You've something else on your mind, haven't you?" God knew of course but wanted Lizzie to say.

"Why couldn't I have been allowed to die after my stroke – it was not living but existing. It was the second most painful time of my life, yet I was in no physical pain, but so much mental anguish?"

"Oh Lizzie, I wanted you to come to Me then, but medical care is now so advanced on the earth that it sometimes interrupts what I want to accomplish".

Father touched her hand and went on:

"I had to wait of course for Molly to speak to you – I was getting her into the right place otherwise you wouldn't be here now. So, you see there was a plan, even with setbacks, I can and do use all things for My good and for the good of those who love Me".

Father and Lizzie looked at each other and Lizzie's love and thanks burst out – "Oh thank You so much for Your love and care, to go to all those lengths to bring me here to be with You. I could dance with joy for all Eternity."

And God said "And so you shall, Lizzie!"

Chapter 3 – Lizzie dances with her Daughter.

Although time in heaven is actually eternity, Lizzie knew that she'd not been in Heaven too long when her friend, Ann found her in her favourite place – practising with the worshippers and dancers in preparation for a special occasion.

"Lizzie, Peter says will you come to the Receiving Room – he's just processing someone he thinks you may be interested in".

"Oh Ann, do you think it could be my daughter, I've not had long to wait have I?"

Peter met them at the door.

"Lizzie, your daughter is here and longing to meet you, but I want to tell you something before you see her. She was born with a disability and has been unable to walk. Her adoptive parents were good to her, but she has had to use a wheelchair all her life. I think you'll find she's not quite used to her new legs just yet". Peter smiled, "You'll have so much to give each other and enjoy together so I'll let you go in now".

Lizzie went in to meet her daughter.

They stood for a while saying nothing – just looking – then Lizzie asked her name.

"It's Jane – Mum". That one word – Mum was all Lizzie needed – she took Jane into her arms, and they hugged and laughed and then talked until Peter had to suggest they went home.

Lizzie suddenly remembered the Celebration that evening when she'd be among the dancers leading the worship.

"Oh, Jane you must stay near me – you'll love it so".

As Lizzie was dancing that evening before God and all the congregation, they were all lost in worship, Lizzie felt someone take her hand – opening her eyes she saw Jane beginning to take her first dancing steps and within seconds she was dancing and leaping before the Throne with her mother and as they looked, could see God's face beaming at them full of love and pride in His creation.

The Twins

Chapter 1 - Twins

The twins were dancing round, they were so excited – today was their naming day. So far they had just been - "the twins", everyone had loved them from the moment they'd arrived, but they had no names – just a boy and a girl from England. Although they were happily dancing and anticipating the coming celebration when they'd arrived five days ago, they were very different.

It was to be a special ceremony the guardians had said the twins had come through a very tough time and needed to feel loved and wanted here.

All the other children always greeted new arrivals and wanted to hear their stories – they listened with compassion and love and when the story was told arms were thrown around and hugs given, and they were then told of the wonderful place they had arrived in and how joyful and happy they would always be here.

When the twins had arrived, somehow there was a quiet hush, everyone knew just by the atmosphere surrounding them that there would be something more horrific in their tale.

The children gathered quietly around the twins and made room in the tall grass filled with wildflowers so that each child was comfortable. Although they knew each time they greeted new arrivals, they would hear dreadful stories, somehow it was necessary before each child could truly experience the wonder of their new Heavenly surroundings.

The boy began - "We thought we might make it into the world alive. As time went on even though we knew we weren't wanted, somehow as each day and month went by, we began to feel slightly safe".

"We were quite old you see". said the girl "nearly seven months".

"Oooooohh" sighed the children – a child called Evie put her arm around the girl.

"Our mum got pushed out of the house when her mum and dad found out she was pregnant, and she wouldn't say who our dad was. She was only 15 and really frightened. We felt it a lot", said the boy.

"She didn't know where to go and walked around for 2 days in the city, sleeping in bus shelters. Nobody came looking for her or asked who she was or where she lived. Then she met some people who helped her to find somewhere to sleep, mostly in shop doorways but sometimes in something called a squat and they protected her as she was so young. She didn't tell them she was pregnant because she thought they'd throw her out.

Anyway, when the weather started to get colder, mum became ill and one of her friends, Matt, got in touch with the social and then we were both taken into care. We were only 5 months old by then and our mum still didn't look pregnant as she was so thin.

When the Care Home found out that she was pregnant and having twins the talking began".

The boy looked at his sister. "You tell the next bit", his voice quavered.

"When you start to hear it's worse – isn't it? Because then you know what's going on and you feel the fear and hear the plans".

The girl stopped and looked across the meadow – she breathed in the scent of the wildflowers around her – it seemed to reassure her that she was only going to have to relive the next part in words only. So, she continued –

"They'd arranged for her to have the operation – we didn't know what it meant, but we began to feel the fear as soon as we arrived at the hospital place.

Our mother was shown into a ward with other girls in. Two were smoking and saying how relieved they'd be when it was all over. Another girl was quietly sobbing into her pillow as the nurse came to fetch her with a trolley. Mum was given a hospital gown so we knew it wouldn't be long and a nurse came with an injection to start the contractions. Soon we felt ourselves being drawn downwards and heard voices talking about their holidays and what they were doing that evening and then the clink of instruments. Somehow my brother found my hand, we must have been fairly close and then we were being pulled apart by some tremendous force which was ripping us apart from each other and from our mother's womb. There was a lot of pain and at the time it must have been unbearable, but as I talk about it here and look around at your faces, I feel no pain in the remembering of it". She looked across at her brother who took her hand and nodded.

Everyone gathered round then, some gathering flowers to adorn their hair, even the boy let them do this, some standing near – no-one said anything for quite a while.

Then Evie (who was so good at welcoming and helping the newcomers to talk through their experiences) said "Look the Guardians are coming, the ceremony is about to start. I wonder what your names will be – I can't wait to know".

The twins held hands as they walked into the centre of the smiling faces and looked up to see the most beautiful smile of all on the face of the One they now knew as their Heavenly Father – they had met Him the moment they arrived and he had welcomed them, sat them on His knee and told them that in a few days' time there would be a huge celebration to name them. Now here they were looking up at Him and feeling the most amazing love and joy that anyone could ever have.

Evie stood near them and whispered in their ears, explaining who people were. That's God and Jesus at His side – look they are both smiling and beckoning for you to get close to them.

The twins went right up to the huge Thrones – they didn't tremble although they knew that these were the most important beings ever –

"You are Peter and Petra" because you both have been very brave, and you will help many more who come here". Their voices sounded as one and the sound was like both thunder and flowing water, mighty and gentle at the same time.

"Peter and Petra" breathed the children "how wonderful, what beautiful names".

God and Jesus raised their hands again "Let the party begin".

Immediately there was music from above and around them all began to dance and sing, waive and dip and bow to God and Jesus, who sat back and smiled and looked and loved all they had made.

Chapter 2 – The Twins Meet Mum

"I think we're losing her" – the voice came through to Beth.

She was drifting now in and out of consciousness – fractured thoughts – where was she? – the emergency room – why? – accident? – God the baby – I'm pregnant" she shouted in her head – "save my baby". Muffled conversation in the distance – then the same voice – "She's pregnant – her boyfriend just told the nurse, 28 weeks – we could try – let's go".

'What's a cinema screen doing in A&E – it's a movie and I'm in it, it's about me! All my favourite memories of childhood, my best friend, Jade and me walking back from school, sharing crisps and sweets. There we are again, this time chatting about boys, how old was I, about 13 there, I think. Who's that boy? Oh, it's Dave, totally forgotten him after all these years. Something about that time, she began living rough on the streets and having her babies stolen.'

On the edge of her mind was something she had to grasp before – before what?... Before she died! Oh God she really was, wasn't she? Something, about God – yes, she'd been to church for a while when she was a teenager, with her friend's mum. "I'd felt really good and happy – before... before...before I lost the twins. Oh God, help me, forgive me, twins wherever you are'.

In Heaven the twins were busy. Suddenly they both stopped and looked up, then at each other.

"Who called us – did you hear that, someone asking our forgiveness". They felt they knew the voice, but it wasn't anyone in Heaven. It was very familiar yet distant. "It's our mother, isn't it?" said Peter "is she on her way here – let's go and look at today's listing of new arrivals.".

They made their way to the Admin area and found Peter and his team so busy they couldn't ask anything but were allowed in the viewing room to see the latest lists.

"It's been such a busy day today – it's holiday time for many people which brings so many road accidents". Bryn, one of Peter's team handed them a list. "Here's an updated list since midday – if you're waiting for someone – there's not a lot of detail, sorry".

Scanning the list, they weren't sure what they were looking for – they didn't know her surname, only that she was Beth. They felt sure they'd know when they spotted her name.

"Here's one about out mum's age – she's arriving with a baby – who they couldn't save – her name's Beth". Peter looked hopeful and beckoned Petra into the viewing area to see if it was her coming towards the gate.

The room was full of expectant family members – all exclaiming as they watched Peter welcome people into Heaven at the Golden gate.

Beth walked tentatively up to the gate, it was just magnificent, the gold, silver and pearl shining the very brightest she'd ever seen, and the light here was so different. Her heart was pounding. "Oh, please may I get into Heaven, I hope I've done everything I need to do, I know I've left it till the very last minute to come in. What will Peter say, what if my name's not in his Book".

Peter smiled down at Beth "And who might you be?" be boomed. He always knew of course who each person was when they approached him, but God felt it was important to identify themselves first to Peter. "I'm Beth and I've had so many surnames that I'm not sure you'll have my name on your list". Beth began to look worried.

Peter opened his book at the page where her latest surname should be. "Ah yes" he beamed "a late entry, but you are clearly here in the Book". Peter reached over with one hand he opened the gates and with his other stroked the head of the baby she carried. "And your baby too, I know you've not had time to name her yet, but you and Father can name her here".

Beth wondered if she could ask Peter the most important question of all. "Yes, Beth" said Peter "your twins are here safely and longing to meet you".

Petra touched Peter's arm, "Look, here is a woman with a baby – I think it's her and look Peter is kissing the baby's face".

"I wonder when we can meet". Peter voiced his thoughts and Bryn who had come into the viewing room said – "These arrivals need a little longer to settle in before seeing families, they'll be meeting with Father first, then we'll arrange a special time for you all".

Peter and Petra walked out and towards the garden area where they sometimes sat enjoying the displays and perfumes of the flowers there. Today though there was an extra dimension to their enjoyment – not just a quiet joy but an exultant bubbling up of excitement as they contemplated seeing their mother's face when they met and meeting another brother or sister, such a lot of eternal joy and fun to look forward to.

Chapter 3 – Beth and God

Beth looked at God, her Heavenly Father in awe. "It still beats me how you can love me just the same as someone like ....Billy Graham or Cliff Richard (who I know isn't here yet)".

God smiled at her.

"That's why we always have this talk with everyone who comes to Heaven, so that you can put everything behind and totally forget as I have. You see as soon as you asked forgiveness – I forgot. It doesn't matter at what stage of your life you do this, and it was a last-minute decision for you, but it is just as valid as say Billy's or Cliff's decisions. It was rubbed out of my memory. You remember of course – but you won't after today – you'll be just the same as Cliff". He smiled.

Beth laughed out loud.

"I heard you had a wonderful reunion with Peter and Petra and they loved little Sally".

"I'm sorry I spent so long away from You on earth – I know I missed so much – I never knew love could be this big". Beth circled her arms to encompass Heaven – "or that there could be such joy and peace".

"I love it too – My perfect plan in operation – a little later than I originally designed but well worth waiting for – here's my son Jesus". He came straight up to Beth and embraced her.

"I love your little ones, they are such fun, We're so pleased you made the right decision in the end. You'd have missed all this forever". Jesus smiled at His Father who had that look in His eye – "And she'd have missed Billy Graham and Cliff – when he arrives". God chuckled.

Ginnys Story

Chapter 1 – Ginny

Bob reached out for Ginny's hand. He didn't squeeze it to ease her anxiety, because he was battling with his own feelings. It was all he could do to reach out to her. The very word amniocentesis had been like a cold, clammy hand on them both since Michael, their doctor gently told them that there was a high-risk factor in a pregnancy at Ginny's age.

Their courtship and marriage was such a surprise for them both. Ginny had become very successful in her profession as Marketing Director in one of the major food outlets and although there had been a few men in her life, she was considered to be totally dedicated to her career. A few years ago, through a family crisis, Ginny found faith in God through the love and support of some friends. She had always thought that Christianity was a sop for the masses and intelligent people like herself had no need for the 'crutch' that religion provided. For goodness sake, there were so many more interesting activities, like theatre, sports, good friends, conversation and music and these diversions were sufficient until that time when the unanswered questions began to surface in her mind.

It was at the church where she met Rob, he too was tentatively reaching out for something more solid in his life and had been persuaded that what he needed was 'God'! He was very wary and when he was invited along to a meal as an introduction to a course exploring the basis of the Christian faith, he had several good excuses and reasons why he wouldn't be able to attend, but somehow, found himself that evening in May 1993 in a very elegant (for a church function, he thought) dining room in someone's home in a 'good' part of London, seated next to a remarkably intelligent woman called Ginny and surrounded by some high city achievers similar to himself.

Many people at the meal, did not come back to attend the course itself, as when its uncompromising nature had been explained, it was not quite the debating forum that many had imagined. Ginny and Rob had stayed, and it was on this 'Alpha' course that they both found a living faith in God through Jesus and also each other, the partner who God had been saving for them.

Their friends were not so sure what to make of the whole affair and for a time thought they had been led into a strange sect at a vulnerable time in their lives, but increasingly, as they saw how the joy and fulfilment that their faith and love for each other enhanced their lives, relaxed and rejoiced with them.

It was not too long after their wedding in June 1994, that Rob and Ginny discovered to their delight that she was pregnant and they felt that God was going to bless their marriage even at this later stage in their lives, with children. Ginny's doctor, however, was not so delighted, he was circumspect at first, waiting to allow Rob and Ginny the time to consider the implications of the possible risks involved. However, in the event he had to spell it out because they were so overjoyed that the risk factor had not even entered their minds. So, it was a massive shock when he gently suggested having the amniocentesis test which could detect abnormalities in the foetus and spoke of his concern for both the foetus and Ginny herself.

Both of them listened to Michael, who was not only their doctor but also a friend, with the dawning realisation that this foetus as Michael called it, was their baby, their embryo, their little person, and that this gentle talk would have to lead to decisions being made for themselves and their child.

So, they sat waiting. The procedure had not been as uncomfortable as she had feared, but this waiting was the worst. Of course, the news would be given by a doctor who didn't know them, couldn't really follow through with any counsel but may give them information which would be life changing for them all.

"Please come through, Mr and Mrs Stanley" the doctor, who introduced himself as Dr Narayev asked them to sit down and performed the usual preliminaries, introducing the nurse who had performed the procedure and going over the reasons why this test was so important.

"I'm sorry" those immortal words which spoke volumes. "The test shows definite abnormalities in the foetus". Dr Narayev presumed this was sufficient information, but Rob queried.

"What does that mean, what are these abnormalities, we realise that you as a doctor might advocate having a termination, but what is the prognosis should Ginny continue with the pregnancy, what specific abnormality have you found?" The questions poured out of Rob.

"The foetus is carrying the Downs Syndrome gene, but there is also a possibility that there may be inadequate development of the heart and lungs for a three-month foetus". Dr Narayev appeared to be a little more amenable after Rob's assertive questioning.

"This is our baby", Ginny could bear this impersonal discussion of her baby no longer "It is not a foetus to us, and," she looked over at Rob "we are going to have this baby".

Rob, swallowed hard, but nodded his head, then gathering himself said "Thank you Doctor for giving us this information, we have made a decision, and I think we always knew that we would continue to have this baby, but now we are a little more informed about the future".

The next few days were very difficult as Ginny and Rob told their friends and family of their decision, they knew they needed the support and prayers of their Christian friends through these next few months. And they received so much love and care that when the birth arrived it was with real anticipation of the forthcoming child, that Rob drove Ginny into St Barts Hospital for the caesarean which had been booked for the following day.

Rob went with Ginny into the operating theatre, standing at her side where he watched the birth of his son. Both of them were overwhelmed with the emotion of the moment at seeing this perfect little person in miniature and with no trace of the facial characteristics of the Downs Syndrome child. They were still marvelling at this while he was being wrapped and weighed and Ginny's post op procedures were being completed, when suddenly the climate in the room changed, and although it was very calmly done, both Ginny and Rob knew there was a problem.

"What is it, is it his heart, lungs?" Rob could see the doctors rushing for some equipment.

"Yes, he's having some difficulty breathing". Their son was rushed into the next room along with all the staff, leaving them momentarily alone.

"Rob, we must pray for him, what shall we call him, he must have a name, God must know what his name is". Ginny's voice with breaking with emotion.

"I think John". Rob said quietly. "Is that OK?".

Ginny nodded, Rob's father had been called John and had been greatly loved by the family, she wished she'd have known him.

They prayed quietly but desperately until a nurse came into the room and told them everything was being done for John at the moment and she would take Ginny back to her room.

It was half an hour before anyone came, and it was Dr Narayev himself who walked into the room.

"Your son is just holding on" he said "but I cannot give you much hope. His heart and lungs are struggling, and we have put him on a ventilator for the moment, but I believe that they are both so undeveloped that they will be unable to support him without a ventilator".

The doctor knew this was the very worst news for any new parent, but he went on to explain the inevitable next steps. We will have to turn the ventilator off but will only do so with your permission and when you are ready. You will want to spend some time with your son".

"John, his name is John" murmured Rob.

Ginny grabbed Rob's hand "We must have him dedicated" and to Dr Narayev. "Do we have time to call our own minister?".

Dr Narayev agreed to this and for whatever time they needed to say both "hello" and "goodbye" to their son.

Rob went outside to phone their Pastor, Neil, who asked if he could bring his wife and Rob went back to find Ginny with their son, holding onto his tiny hand through the incubator sleeves.

It was such a bitter-sweet service. Neil and Sylvie had become good friends and their sadness mixed with the continued grief of Ginny and Rob at this simple service of dedication was very poignant, knowing he would very shortly be with God. At the end of the service, Neil gently asked them if they wanted to say something to John, and they both told him how much they'd wanted him and that they loved him and so, so sad that he wouldn't have any life with them on earth. They told him that he would be happy with God, and they would see him there.

They decided that while they were all together, they would have the life support machine switched off and Neil would commit him to God as he died.

The doctor came in and simply flicked a switch and left the room, there was nothing he could say, but his demeanour spoke of a quiet sympathy.

John arrived at 10.30am on Monday 2nd September and left at 3.30pm, just five hours old.

But, as he entered Heaven and was greeted by the children at the gates, he knew himself to have been loved and wanted for even such a short time. And now he was going to wait here for mummy and daddy to arrive, but until then he would enjoy finding out about such things as playing and learning. He'd have such things to tell them.

Chapter 2 – John's Life

John grew in Heaven from the tiny little mite who'd arrived, into a strong young man who St. Peter himself chose for his right-hand man. He loved his work from the very moment he awoke from a sleep that was never needed but simply a God-given pause in the work and a time of refreshment. He'd run to the Admin Centre by the gates to join Peter, who had his apartment there, ready to prepare for the day's entrants.

Peter was so pleased with him, he'd had very many helpers over the centuries, and as was the way in Heaven they moved round into some other form of service, to allow for variety and enjoyment, but John learned so quickly. Of all the thousands of assistants' he'd known, John's smile beamed out the widest at every person who entered the gates, wide-eyed with excitement and yet nervous with awe and wonder and he would stand behind Peter at the welcome and just beam with joy and love, putting every new entrant at ease.

He would talk with Peter during their brief times of quiet, sitting on a grassy hill which overlooked the Heavenly gates in one direction and the Golden Street into the City in the other. They talked about many things, about Peter's life on earth with Jesus, what they'd done, who and what they'd seen. Also, about Peter's early life as a child by the Lake of Galilee and his days as a fisherman before Jesus had called Peter to follow Him. He especially enjoyed the stories about Jesus stilling the storm and walking on the water and Peter never tired of telling, making each story as fresh as the day it happened.

They'd talked of John's mum and dad and Peter told him all he knew of them, that they'd been very sad for a long while after he'd come to Heaven, but that they were happy now and had been foster parents to many children over the years. Peter told John that they talked of him often and how they looked forward to meeting with him in Heaven. John spoke often of that day and of meeting with all the children who they'd fostered, he knew he'd love them too as brothers and sisters as his mum and dad loved them, and he'd have lots to ask them about their lives too.

Chapter 3 – Ginny and John

John was almost incoherent with excitement Peter just laughed as John jumped up and down every time the lights on the gates flashed with the approach of a newcomer.

"John", laughed Peter "you can see who is approaching on the CCTV screen, your mum is the next one due in".

John sat at the monitor peering so closely, hoping to see even further down the approach road than the camera could reach.

"Here she is Peter". John watched as the faint outline became a recognisable figure of a woman and then John was able to see her features for the very first time.

"She looks just like me, Peter". John was amazed. "Well, she is your mother", chuckled Peter going out of the office to prepare for the opening of the Gates.

"Well, are you coming or are you going to continue watching on the screen". Peter smiled as he held open the door for John who was having difficulty keeping behind Peter.

Every step for Ginny had been easier than the last. At first as she stepped out of her life on earth, the steps had been heavy, but as she now approached the Gates of Heaven, she knew she could run. Her thoughts had been centred on meeting God and Jesus and being with them forever, but meeting her son for the first time would be so wonderful.

The Gates swung open and there stood Peter, how majestic he looked, whatever must God be like she wondered. Just behind Peter stood a man a little shorter than him, but quite impressive and with a lovely smile.

"Welcome Ginny", Peter took her hand and led her through the gates. "We've been waiting for you, your name is here, and John here has checked you in, so please come in".

"John?" Ginny's voice trembled a little, "Not my John?"

"Yes" Peter stood back to allow John to step forward and they fell into each other's arms.

"I'll let your son show you around and explain everything to you. He can take you to meet Father and show you where you will live in Heaven. He can have some holiday time – he's been looking forward to this day forever!"

Chapter 4 – John, God and Mum

John realised that he was being given something very special when Peter called him to say that God had decided that he, John, should be the one to take his mum to meet with Him.

Ginny knew this day was going to the very best in all eternity. For the first time she would really see God and Jesus who she had loved from the very first moment she had met Him on earth and her own son John would be there too.

As they entered the Hall, John marvelled again at the magnificence of it. Of course, he had not seen anything like it on earth, but he knew that there would not have been anything to compare with this. John's heart was bursting with love as he walked with his mum up to the Throne. Even in Heaven it was not possible to look into God's face straight away, it had to be done slowly, starting with His feet and over his shimmering robes and lastly to His face.

God extended his arm towards Ginny and with his other drew His Son, Jesus towards her, Ginny fell at His feet and Jesus tenderly lifted her up.

"I understood your pain at losing John, this is My Son who I had to give up for a time". God smiled and put his arm around His Son and Jesus smiled up at Him a smile so full of worship that it lit up the already brilliant room until it seemed as if their faces were of burnished gold.

God then explained to Ginny how even though He knew how much it would hurt her to lose John, He had a special purpose and task for him in Heaven and told her of John's unique position as special assistant to Peter.

Ginny had often felt proud of her foster children who did well and indeed, loved them all, but this surely overshadowed all that as her heart filled with love and joy for her first-born son.

"How Rob will enjoy this when he arrives". Ginny looked forward to a wonderful eternity as she beamed back at God, Jesus and John.

Irene

Chapter 1 - Irene's Baby

"Do you remember Irene?" Val asked her friend, Sue. Several vivid memories sprang to her mind.

"I didn't know her as well as you, but she was very lost in her own world until she hooked onto something, then she wouldn't let go. – I remember she had a very strong will".

Val looked across the bus at the woman who had drawn that memory out of her and thought back to the time 6 years ago when she had been involved in Irene's life.

Irene had wandered into church one Sunday and sat on the front row – rocking backwards and forwards for most of the service.

As Val had sat down next to her after the service, Irene said "Isn't the music lovely? It really makes me feel happy. I can hear the voices in my head you know, but no-one believes me". She went on to tell Val about her specific type of mental illness and the medication she was on which caused her to act the way she did, and Val was totally surprised by Irene's very lucid and intelligent conversation.

Val had then begun to visit Irene at her home and met with her Community Nurse who came to administer the weekly injections, as Irene was notorious for not turning up at the Clinic for her medication or altering the dosage. Val had spent many hours at different times with Irene attempting to help her see which of her fears and phobias were real and which imagined and sometimes Val thought she had a breakthrough when Irene would be able to see herself clearly.

During times of stability Val enjoyed their times together when she was slighter better. She would take her wool for Irene's compulsive knitting. Irene would sit in her rocking chair knitting furiously and her cat, (when it chose to live with her, as she didn't always feed it,) would bat the wool around the room. They'd talk about the places she'd been to earlier in her life, but there were so few subjects which weren't fraught with the danger of triggering some deep emotion and sending her into a paranoidal spiral. There were also times when she was extremely sociable and would take herself off to the pub or social club and it was here that she met Jim.

Val met Jim when she called round one morning and she immediately knew that Jim was not after Irene's best interests.

"Hi Jim", Val knew she must give him a chance even though her initial reaction was one of recoil.

"Huh", Jim grunted. His gaze took in Val's clothes and shoes and then he noticed the shopping bag with her purse balancing on the top of some fruit.

"Shall I make coffee?" Val volunteered.

"S'alright" muttered Jim, we've got some tinnies". He pointed to the six pack of lager which were now four. It was 9.30am!

But Val knew she could not protect Irene from her own choice, and it shortly became obvious that they were sleeping together, and Irene was very vague when Val mentioned birth control or safe sex.

When Irene began complaining of losing her appetite, Val suggested a visit to the doctor, but Irene was adamant – they were not to be trusted. So, Val bought a pregnancy kit and with much trepidation, suggested Irene used it. It was positive and jolted Irene into a state of rosy haziness.

"Jim will marry me", she was very sure that all would be well and was happily planning her wedding.

Jim scarpered quicker than a ferret down a hole and Irene's mental state plummeted drastically. Within days of Jim's departure, she had barred the doors against her nurse, social worker and even Val.

She would not even answer the phone and although Val could see her through the sitting room curtains huddled before the electric fire, she would not open her door but had a faraway look.

The police had to be called of course – the social worker shouted through Irene's letter box that they were going to have to break down her door. It was awful, all the neighbours crowding round or peering through their net curtains watching the action.

"I've not seen her out for days", said the lady who lived opposite – "and she hasn't properly opened her curtains for a week".

Her immediate neighbour had a more worrying report. "She's been talking loudly to someone at all hours of the day and night" – but I've not seen anyone come or go! She's really round the twist, isn't she?"

Karen, her new social worker turned up – another different key worker – that wouldn't help Irene, she wouldn't be able to trust anyone she didn't know! She shouted through the letter box. "Come on Irene, be a good girl and open the door or we'll have to break it down".

"Irene", Val tapped on the window so that Irene could see her. "Please open up – I've got some cat food and some knitting wool".

She continued this conversation to try and diffuse the situation. "How's the cat – is he in there with you?" There was no response and half an hour later the police made a decision to break in. It was a reasonably clean break in and in fact it hardly startled Irene at all, as she sat by the fire hunched up with her hand around her belly and talking to the baby.

"We'll have some lovely times you and I". she was saying "You don't have to have a daddy – we'll have each other, and I'll buy you some pretty clothes and a springy pram and get a dog or a hamster". It broke our hearts to hear her and see how much she longed for the life she was describing to her baby.

"Irene", Karen her social worker bent down and spoke gently to Irene. "We'll have to section you, you know that don't you, for yourself and for the baby".

Irene did know – she'd been sectioned often enough to know it was inevitable that she'd be taken into hospital for her own good and especially now for the baby. So, she sighed, standing up, and really, she welcomed this when it came as it gave her some respite from the responsibility of having to think at all.

Val visited her next day in the special ward – she couldn't find her at first but located her talking to a man in the day room about Jim and her expected baby. She gently touched Irene's shoulder. "Hello Irene" she said

"Oh Val, this is Ken, I'm just telling him about my new baby. You'll have to visit when I'm home, Ken".

It was a depressing visit, Val felt Irene had completely lost touch with reality and had to be helped back to bed as her last dose of medication kicked in and she whoozed out of it. Val attempted to find out what the prognosis was for Irene and her baby – but she wasn't family, and therefore not included in any case conferences or entitled to any information other than the statutory answer: - "We are doing everything we can in the situation".

Val very frustrated stormed out of the hospital.

"What are You doing God?", she flung at the sky. "I feel so helpless".

She phoned Karen when she reached home. "Is there any way she can keep the baby, perhaps with help?" Val knew even as she was asking this, that there was no other way, that society could not offer the help that Irene needed, and felt so guilty that she herself couldn't help. She knew what the outcome would be.

It was four days later that Val found out about the termination of Irene's pregnancy.

She visited Irene and was not surprised to find her totally uncommunicative, and she stared at Val out of drugged eyes that were sunk in despair. 'Why?' they seemed to say.

Val often wondered if she could have altered the course of things – if she should have fought to be informed as a close friend of the medical decision which had been taken for Irene and prevented the termination of the pregnancy by offering to foster the baby. With hindsight she knew that this was through a sense of guilt and frustration at not being able to offer any real help.

Val lost touch with Irene soon after her discharge from hospital. The medication had stabilised her sufficiently to allow her home and during this period she made a decision to move to another area. They kept in touch by phone for a time then Val found she'd moved again and had no forwarding address or phone number.

As Val's thoughts adjusted themselves into the present – she saw with a start that the woman who'd so reminded her of Irene was stepping off the bus – she had a small child with her and with a start Val realised that Irene's child would have been about this age.

Val would go to the cemetery on Sunday and place some flowers there for the unknown baby and for Irene wherever she was now.

Chapter 2 – Tara's Story

When people arrived in Heaven they came whole – healed of whatever, but still everyone was amazed at little Tara, the tiny foetus had been nearly all Valium, but still she arrived a tiny, lively, bouncing, chuckling child.

She was so active – her guardian, Helen covered a few Heavenly miles trying to find Tara. She was interested in everything – she'd soon outgrown the creche – when she'd flown over the walls, trying out her new wings, even though they weren't fully formed. Today, Helen found her in the White Robe room. Tara was watching the light playing on the gold threads used to stitch the robes.

"Oh, Helen, I'd love to work here when I'm bigger, can I? Look at the lovely gold and white robes". Tara's words fell over themselves in her excitement.

"Yes, I'll put your name on that list for when you're old enough. Now don't fly off straight away. I've something to tell you".

"What, what is it? Am I seeing Father again, I love Him so much"? Tara's eyes widened in anticipation.

"No, but something nearly as good, your mother has arrived here very suddenly, we didn't know she was coming until an hour ago".

Tara sat down with a bump. Her mum! She'd been told the story of course, how her mum was not well and had a poorly head and she knew she often took a lot of pills.

"Did she get run over by a car or bus, then?" questioned Tara.

"No", Helen would have to explain this in language Tara could understand while she was still so young. "Tara, your mum couldn't remember how many pills to take and swallowed too many. They stopped her heart from beating and she died". Helen looked at Tara's face to see her reaction. It was half concern and half excitement.

"I really think she wanted to come here soon to meet you". said Helen.

"My mum, I'm going to meet my mummy". Tara quietly crooned the words like a little song to herself.

"Would you like me to bring her to meet you – I know she wants to meet her baby girl".

Tara sat waiting. She'd found it hard to sit quietly but Helen was helping her and now she'd see her mummy.

In the distance, Tara recognised a lady in a pink and white dress – "That's my mummy". She wanted to fly but thought she might fly too high and go right over her – or land on top of her!"

As she drew nearer Irene's face changed for the second time since she'd arrived in Heaven. First, when she'd met Father, her features (formerly drawn and haggard) had undergone the best ever face-lift and the look of a pill junkie wiped away in an instant. Now her face was shining.

She beamed "Oh, my daughter, my lovely daughter, Tara". She opened her arms and Tara wasn't sure if she ran into her mum's or flew there, she loved her wings so.

Helen tiptoed way leaving them talking and laughing together, wrapped in each other's arms.

Chapter 3 – An End to Anguish

Irene had been inseparable from Tara since her arrival in Heaven but today was different. She was going to talk to God. Would He really understand her life, would He be able to make some sense out of its senselessness? She was so glad she was here and simply couldn't see anything good in looking back to her life on earth.

She walked into God's Presence Room and gave a sharp intake of breath. Around the room were pictures of her throughout her life. She ran over to one of her childhood. "Oh, look Father", she said "that's one of me with my best friend, Kerry".

Father came and stood beside her.

"Can you remember what happened that day?" God gently prodded her memory.

"Ooh yes", memory stirred in Irene. "Kerry fell into the brook when we were playing, and I pulled her out".

"You had to go in quite deep didn't you" said Father "and you weren't scared, all you were thinking about was getting Kerry out because she'd fallen on her face. Do you know you saved her life, if you'd gone for help, she'd have drowned? Her mother wanted to thank you, but you'd moved away".

Irene's eyes widened, she hadn't known she'd really saved Kerry's life.

"Here's a more recent photo of you". Father pointed to one of Irene in hospital.

"Why is that here, I wasn't good there, I was very difficult and wouldn't take my medication. I was such a headache to the staff. Kept threatening to discharge myself".

"Can you see the girl in the next bed?" asked Father.

"Oh yes", that was Susie, she'd slashed her wrists badly and the nurses thought she'd die. But she didn't. Irene suddenly remembered a conversation she'd had with Susie when she'd woken the next day.

"Susie had been moaning and sobbing about wanting to be left to die and I told her she was selfish, cos she'd got a lovely husband and child and that You would help her get over her attempted suicide".

"And I did" said Father emphatically, "She's still alive on earth, a happy Christian lady with a lovely family. Do you know she tells many people about how you spoke to her that day? Gave her hope. You see Irene, your life was not in vain, but I'm so glad you're here with Me now".

Irene nodded.

"It was a life of anguish. I couldn't cope with even the small things of life, so I opted out into mental turmoil. I'm glad I'm here too Father".

Helen came to fetch Irene but tiptoed away as Father was holding Irene close to His heart and telling her how useful she was going to be to Him in Heaven.

Carol and Jim's Story

Chapter 1 - Carol and Jim

Jenny read the headlines -TEENAGER FOUND IN WOOD and quickly read the paragraph to find out if the girl had been named. She hoped it wasn't Carol. Carol's mother had called some months ago to let her know Carol had left home and she was worried about her lifestyle.

Now aged 14, she had been a very difficult teenager but then her mother had many problems too and their relationship had never been very good.

She read on –

'A girl has been found in a local wooded area last evening. This is being treated as a murder investigation and evidence of a sexual attack has been found'.

It went on to give the name of the girl as Carol Ann Hardy, a local girl. Her mother was pictured being comforted by a policewoman.

Jenny felt sick, she'd lost contact with the family over the years and had wondered how they were, but 'murder'. Poor, sad little Carol, always ready to please, yet always in trouble. She felt a combination of emotions, guilt because she hadn't kept in touch, anger at a system which failed to meet Carol and Jim's needs, and such a great sadness overwhelmed her as her imagination played a scenario of how she might have died.

Jenny dialled Mary's number – no reply. She would try later on and offer to go round. She'd no idea where Jim, Carol's brother was these days. Jim was older than Carol, he would be around 20 now and Jenny presumed he was off and away from his hometown.

She began to remember how she'd first come into contact with the family.

Mary had approached her one Sunday about 7 years ago at the church bookstall and within two minutes had told Jenny her entire family's history. All of it came pouring out from the pending court case of a neighbour for the regular sexual abuse of Carol and Jim while baby-sitting. Also, her ex-husband subjecting the children to watch himself and his girl-friend having sex. And not surprisingly the misconduct of the children at school. Her own difficulties paled into insignificance next to her children's, but she did have problems of her own too.

Carol and Jim were loving children, very tactile and also very vulnerable. Even when talking and playing with Jenny they displayed behaviour of a maturity beyond their childish ages. They would sit very close together giggling and tickling each other, getting sillier and sillier.

Jenny knew their story and although she wanted to part them and stop their game, she knew that the responsibility was not hers and she had no authority to step in and help. It broke her heart, but all she could do was offer her support to their mum and occasionally listen to Carol or just hug her.

Jenny had visited the family and taken them out, ferried them around for parties or school functions and generally began to gain some trust from the children. Their social worker too trusted Jenny with information and some progress was made.

Until another incident happened totally beyond Jenny's comprehension. A very close and trusted friend committed further abuse on both the children who by this time were fully versed in the ways of secrecy to this type of behaviour and this only became known when Carol began exhibiting strange behaviour at school. She then disclosed all that had been happening to them both yet again.

Jenny's eyes filled with tears as she remembered how Carol had loved the music in church – she'd sit transfixed, a look of pure delight on her face, almost a radiance.

What devasted Jenny was the knowledge that these children had grown up thinking that this behaviour was normal between adults and children. Such a futile life – what joy or hope did Carol and Jim ever have.

Jenny went the way of condemning herself for a time. That she hadn't done more, said more, prayed more. If only, she sat thinking. It didn't do any good, thinking like that she knew, but how different their life could and indeed should have been. Carol's, at any rate. Jim hopefully still had half a chance to change. She'd pray for him wherever he was now.

Chapter 2 – A Life in Four Acts

Carol didn't feel the final blow when it came, nor mercifully what followed.

She was a child again and back in that fearful caravan of her 'Uncle's' garden. The family party was happening just yards from where her uncle had led her to 'show her something special – our secret'.

She was feeling, hearing and seeing again all the sounds and impressions which had drastically coloured her 6-year-old life. There were 12 rivets in the roof of the caravan above her head, she was good at sums, so she began looking for other things to count. The sound of the gas lights as they 'pop – popped', a kind of musical beat, the chatter and laughter going on only a shout away. But uncle had also said "don't let anyone know about this – you'll get into a lot of trouble if you tell of our secret".

She began to fasten her hopes on that gas light. 'If it goes out, uncle will have to go back inside, and anyway mummy must have missed me and come looking – she'll shout me soon to come in'. But mummy didn't shout, the gas light didn't go out and uncle had led her to that caravan many times over the next few years.

The scene changed and the feelings disappeared as if a heavy curtain had closed on Act 1, Scene 1 and suddenly it was the interval. She could hear music, not the plastic, piped music of the cinemas and shopping centres, but so beautiful as if her heart would explode with warmth.

The as quickly as Act 1 had faded, Act 2 began.

Her bedroom. She was seven years old. Since her father had left her mum, he'd had a succession of 'aunties' and mum began going out each Friday to a local club. Her friend's 19-year-old son had offered to babysit Carol and Jim. Again, vivid sounds and impressions came, Jim shouting something from his room, it sounded muffled, maybe one of his fighting games. Later as she saw her door opening, she knew what would follow and with an adult life experience in a 7-year-old's head she knew what Jim's calls had been about. The baby-sitter was a hefty young man who 'worked out' and her mum never understood (or didn't want to) why Carol objected every Friday and made what her mum said was 'such a fuss'.

Again, that interval music – what was it? - she couldn't hold on to it long enough – but that wonderful feeling flooding over her.

The next scene was much more painful because it had made more of an impression and changed forever her trust in adults. A bedroom in her father's house. She was now 8 years-old. She and Jim stayed with their father occasionally. His voice calling her and Jim into his bedroom, making them sit at the foot of the bed while he and his 'girl-friend' of the moment performed their own grotesque acts.

She wanted to close her eyes on this scene, to bring once again that soothing peace of the music.

She heard it faintly, but her immediate attention was captured by the large, high space she was in. A dappled, coloured light filtered from long windows falling onto stone pillars and wooden furniture, the shimmering, coloured gold and brass reflecting candles, the music increased in volume and intensity.

'Ahh,' Carol remembered St. Peter's church where her mum had gone for a while, and they'd met Jenny. 'Oh, Jenny', Carol's eyes pricked with tears as she remembered Jenn's hugs. The music was now filled with words – she recognised – songs about Jesus. She loved looking at the stained glass in the church – Jesus depicted as the shepherd, particularly held Carol. She gazed longingly at the shepherd as He gathered his sheep and lambs with his crook, such a loving look on his face, it made her heart ache.

The music swelled into a song she'd heard "Jesus take me as I am I can come no other way".

Then another shutter came down.

Act 4 was more recent and was what her life had become. Carol and her friend Margie standing on the street corner waiting for the tell-tale slowing of the cars and the whispered conversation through the car window, then a hurried tussle in the back of the car or in a seedy hotel. Then back to the street to continue her chat with Margie or another street worker while waiting to earn the next few pounds.

They knew it was a risky profession – if it wasn't the fear of some disease, it was an even worse fear of a nasty attack resulting in a visit to A&E. But death – No, not Carol, she was too canny.

Where was that music coming from now? It seemed all around her and that voice singing, sounded so.... almost angelic! It was very loud now, in her ears. It was her own voice and as she sang her heart warmed fit to burst, like hugging kittens. Was this love? Her head and eyes felt funny too – a dazzling bright light which formed itself into a person walking towards her. Her stomach clenched – its not dad is it?

With a jolt like a bolt of lightning going through her heart she recognised him because He held his cross and smiled towards her as if she were a sheep or a lamb.

It was Jesus. He'd come for her.

Chapter 3 – Not a Futile Life

Peter was surprised. Very, very rarely did Jesus Himself come to the Gates of Heaven. In fact, Peter knew of only 5 occasions when Jesus had opened the Gates Himself to meet and welcome in that very special person – that person who Peter knew, needed to have God's love and assurance immediately.

He wondered which one of the many expected today Jesus might be meeting. He looked at his computer screen, no well-known International Leader was expected, maybe it was an important Person who'd made a death-bed commitment.

Jesus waved to Peter through the window and gestured that He'd open the Gates. He realised that Jesus was carrying his shepherd's crook. He'd not seen that since…….. Oh Peter's eyes and heart burned with such a fresh love as he played over in his mind some of their times on earth 2000 odd years ago – it didn't seem like even 20 years ago.

Peter came down to watch as Jesus' hand rested on the latch of the Golden Gate (it was made of solid gold and pearls and so heavy, but it always amazed Peter that it swung open so easily at the lightest touch). It opened slowly to reveal the path beyond.

Just turning the corner was the slight figure of a girl and even as Peter watched he was thrilled afresh to see that with each step nearer to Heaven her whole being, body and face were being changed.

At the corner she was carrying a great burden on her back, her shoulders, hands and all around her waist were tied great weights, but with each step the weights fell off, then she dropped the heavy loads in her hands. As her eyes caught sight of the gates (she couldn't yet see who'd opened them) the load fell off her shoulders.

Suddenly she was near enough for Peter to see her face and as always, the expression on the faces of new arrivals at their first glimpse of their Saviour was a sight even the angels rejoiced to see.

She would have been about 20 yards away when she saw Him.

Every step had been a relieving of pain but her back still hurt her. She lifted her eyes to see how far the gate was, at her first sighting she had thought it was a mirage, it was so bright and shining but when she blinked to clear her vision the bright light became a person, a person she felt she recognised.

Who did she know in Heaven who would meet her at the gate? She'd not known many 'good' people at all and even though she'd got this far wasn't sure she'd be allowed in. Perhaps it was the Recording Angel and she'd have to think up some excuse as to why she'd come up this path. THEN she saw it – the crook in His hand.

"Jesus" she whispered – then "Jesus" she shouted and began to run the last few yards. With the shout two things happened, the last of that heavy load fell off her back and Jesus opened His arms for her to run into. He lifted her and spun her round laughing. "Hello, Carol, welcome to heaven, your new home.

Peter watched, awed once again as the King of Kings and Lord of Lords walked slowly hand in hand, lovingly reassuring the new arrival that, "Yes", she was in the right place – her name had been written here since the beginning and events in her life had prevented her from knowing that, that she'd be safe and would find a happiness she'd never known.

Peter also knew that in time God would explain to Carol how He'd cried with her at life's hurts, then He'd let her talk and ask Him many things. He'd tell her she would see Jim again – that they'd eventually be reunited and enjoy Heaven together with a pure love.

Peter sat down and looked at the screen. What a refreshing change from the welcome of some lifelong believer, however wonderful that always was, they knew what to expect. Carol's absolute amazement that the Jesus who she'd only seen in a stained-glass window was now showing her around His Heaven.

'Oh yes, it was even better than listening to the Angelic Choir'.

www.ingramcontent.com/pod-product-compliance
Lightning Source LLC
Chambersburg PA
CBHW070056120526
44588CB00033B/1647